PETERHOF

NINA VERNOVA
VADIM ZNAMENOV

PETERHOF

ABRIS ART PUBLISHERS

ST PETERSBURG · PETERHOF

2003

CONTENTS

*I. Chesky after a drawing by M. Shotoshnikov.
View of the Samson Pool with Fountains and
Cascades in the Lower Gardens at Peterhof. 1810s*

INTRODUCTION

The marble obelisk standing near the railing of the Upper Park in Peterhof bears the incised numbers *26* and *29*. The first one indicates the distance from St Petersburg in *versts* and the second in kilometres. The obelisk shows the distance from the old border of St Petersburg at the Obvodny Canal to the splendid suburban residence of the Russian Emperors and now the world-famous palace and park museum complex, the "capital of fountains" Peterhof.

Peterhof is located on the southern coastland of the Gulf of Finland. The area of its parks created in the course of two centuries is about 1000 hectares. Two of them, the oldest Lower Park and the nineteenth-century Alexandria, stretch along the shore of the Gulf of Finland. The sea in this place had receded to its present-day borders little by little forming terraces at the shoreline. This specific character of the terrain made it possible to lay out parks at two levels.

At different times, starting from the period of its foundation by Peter the Great as an official summer residence, more than ten palaces and a large number of elegant garden pavilions have been put up at Peterhof. The creation of a unique fountain system made it possible to decorate the parks of the imperial residence with more than 150 fountains.

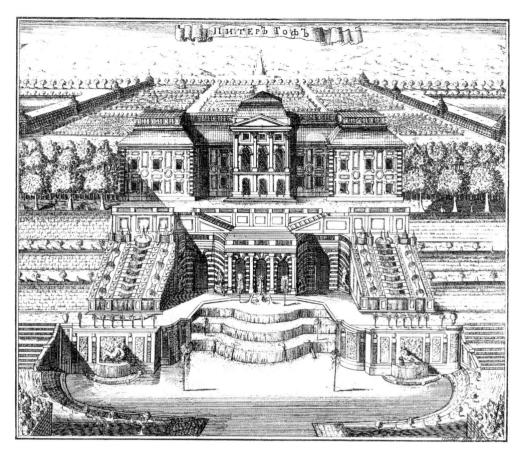

ПИТЕРГОФЪ

A. Rostovtsev. The Great Cascade and the Upper Mansion. 1717. Engraving

*G. Kneller. Portrait of Peter the Great.
Early 18th century* ▶

In May 1703 Peter the Great founded in the mouth of the Neva, on the territory fought back from the Swedes, the city of St Petersburg that would become the new capital of Russia. To defend the city from the sea the construction of the Kronslot citadel (the forerunner of the famous Crohnslott Fortress). Peter often visited the construction site. He reached it by sea or, in case of bad weather, by land along the southern coast of the gulf. There was a farmstead on the shore called Pieterhof or "Peter's Court" in the Dutch manner (the present-day spelling "Peterhof" was introduced much later). The first mention of Peterhof appeared in the *Field Journal* of Peter the Great on 13 September 1705, but the idea to create a suburban royal residence there would emerge later. It was only in 1714 that the building of the Upper Chambers (the future Great Palace) and the Palace of Monplaisir to the east of it, on the seashore, began. At the same time a canal was being dug out from the sea to the foot of the terrace, over which the construction of the Upper Chambers was under way. Simultaneously the park was being laid out in the lower part of the area. It became known as the Lower Park to differentiate it from the Upper Park or Kitchen Garden laid out behind the Upper Chambers.

The first general plan of Peterhof was drawn up by Johann Friedrich Braunstein in 1716. The construction of the Marly Palace began in 1720. By that time not only the western border of the park had been determined, but the architectural centre of the area had been shaped with a trident of avenues running from it and crossing the Lower Park from west to east. In a year the Hermitage Pavilion was founded on the seashore in the western part of the park, symmetrically to Monplaisir. The slanting avenue leading to it together with the slanting alley running from the Upper Chamber to Monplaisir and the Sea Canal formed another trident linking the terrace with the sea. Thus the basic network of avenues in the area came into being. The Lower Park was laid out as a typical regular park in the French taste. All the work there was supervised by the master gardener Leonard van Harnichfelt invited from Holland.

Despite all the difficulties in the construction work connected with a severe climate and floods, the Lower Park with its drainage system, flower-beds, pools and fountain structures produced a strong impression on the guests of Peterhof as early as 1723. Thus the French ambassador Campredon wrote to Louis XV that the progress in the construction of the residence was "truly amazing". He also quoted the words of Peter the Great who said to him during the demonstration of the park from the balcony of the Upper Chambers: "You at Versailles haven't got such beautiful view as this – the sea and Kronstadt on one side and St Petersburg on the other."

It was not a mere chance that Peter the Great chose this site for the construction of Peterhof. Investigating the locality to the south of the future summer residence, he discovered several water reservoirs fed by underground springs at the distance of about twenty kilometres from it, near the villages of Kipen and Ropsha. The creation of the water-supply system was entrusted to the Russian hydraulic engineer Vasily Tuvolkov who was taught in Holland and France. Under his guidance a canal and sluices were built during the summer of 1721 and water began to flow from Ropsha Hills by gravity to the storage pools in the Upper Gardens. However, the system made it possible to create only small jets of water there. The Lower Park which extended at the foot of the large terrace was more favourable for fountain building. Water stored in the reservoirs of the Upper Gardens, when released, rushed down through the pipes from the height of sixteen meters according to the law of communicating vessels to erupt in a great number of high streams of water in the fountains of the Lower Park. The principles of water supply found by Peter the Great are still used today testifying to the Emperor's engineering talent.

The construction of the fountains and the improvement of the fountain system continued with intervals until the middle of the

10

Unknown mid-18th-century artist.
The Large Palace at Peterhof. Engraving

nineteenth century. As a result a large-scale complex has been formed including more than one hundred and fifty fountains and four cascades in the Lower Park and five fountains and one cascade in the Upper Gardens. The Peterhof fountains are unparalleled in the world practice of fountain art in terms of artistic and engineering solution, diversity of design, abundance of water and functioning period.

The ceremony of the inauguration of Peterhof – the first festivity in the royal residence – was held on 15 August 1723. By this time a group of fountains was already functioning, the decoration of the Upper Chambers and Monplaisir finished, the construction of the Marly Palace was over and the Hermitage was basically built.

With the death of Peter the Great and his wife Catherine I two years later the construction of the suburban residence came to a halt. A true flowering of Peterhof started only under Empress Elizabeth Petrovna, Peter's daughter. It was in her reign that the archi-

tect Francesco Bartolomeo Rastrelli reconstructed the Upper Chambers into the luxurious Great Palace and designed new fountains.

In 1762 Peterhof witnessed the events connected with the overthrow of Peter III and the proclamation of his wife Empress Catherine II. Paul I, who succeeded Catherine on the throne, focused his attention on the core of Peterhof created in the reign of Peter the Great. By his orders the lead statues of the Great Cascade were replaced by bronze ones; Andrei Voronikhin erected majestic colonnades at the flower-beds of the Great Parterres and had a beautiful fountain group, *Neptune*, installed in the Upper Park. This period of turbulent innovation, however, did not last long. The active construction work at Peterhof was resumed only twenty-five years later, during the period of the reign of Nicholas I. In 1826 the Alexandria Park was laid out to the east of the Lower Park. The architect Adam Menelaws put up the Cottage Palace for the imperial family there as well as the palatial church, the so-called Gothic Chapel, designed by Karl Friedrich Schinkel, nearby. Not far from the Gothic Chapel Menelaws built the Farm re-

designed later by Andrei Stakenschneider into the Farm Palace of Alexander II and his family.

The second half of the nineteenth century saw a gradual decline of Peterhof. It was only in the reign of Nicholas II that the work revived and the architect Anton Tomishko built the last Peterhof palace, the Lower Dacha, on the shore of the Gulf of Finland in Alexandria.

Throughout its existence Peterhof has accumulated immense cultural values. Its parks – the Upper Gardens and Lower Park – are decorated with magnificent statuary and its palaces concentrate fine collections of painting, sculpture, furniture, bronze, porcelain and glass. After the Revolution of 1917 more than a dozen of palaces and pavilions of Peterhof have been converted into museums of Russian and Western European art of the early eighteenth to the early twentieth century.

The most difficult time in the life of the former royal residence were the years of the Nazi occupation during the Second World War. Many works of architecture were destroyed, the parks were pitted with trenches and dug-outs, the fountain system was wrecked. The sculptures of the Great Cascade which had not been removed to safety – *Samson*, the *Neva*, the *Volkhov* and *Tritons* – were stolen. At the Nuremberg Trials the destruction of Peterhof was condemned as a crime against humanity.

The restoration work in the capital of fountains began soon after the liberation of Peterhof. Already on 17 June 1945 the ceremony of the opening of the Lower Park took place and during the next summer the first fountains began to function. With the bringing into operation of the Lion Cascade in the western part of the park in August 2000 the restoration of the fountain structures in the Lower Park has been completed.

The opening of the summer season which is celebrated every year at the end of May in the presence of many thousands of guests is a fascinating and memorable pageant. The fountains begin to spurt out jets of water again after their winter "repose" bringing joy to everybody who comes to see the marvel of Peterhof, a place which will never lose its aura of beauty and poetic mystery.

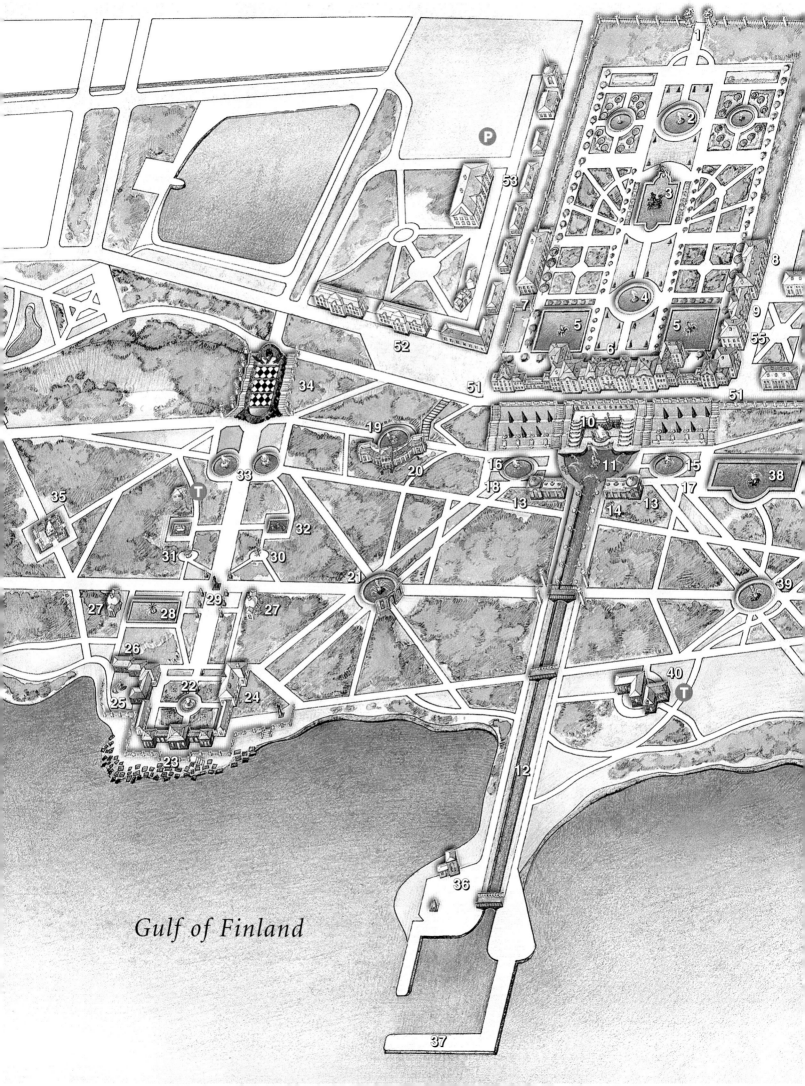

Gulf of Finland

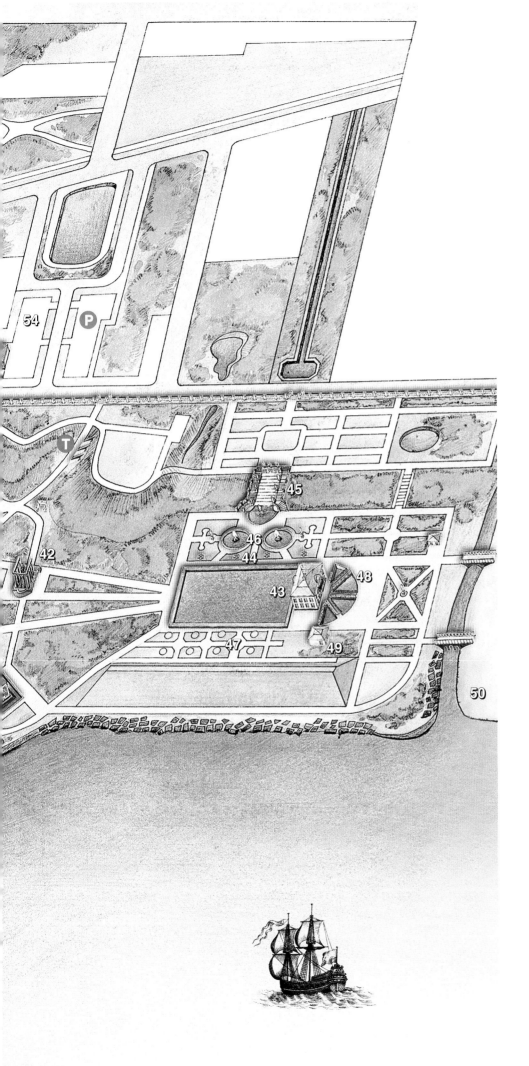

THE UPPER GARDENS

1. *The Main Gates. The main entrance*
2. *The Mezheumny (Indefinite) Fountain*
3. *The Neptune Fountain*
4. *The Oak Fountain*
5. *The fountains of the Square Pools*
6. *The Great Palace Museum*
7. *The Upper Gardens Mansion. The Museum of Private Collections*
8. *The Department of Museum Parks*
9. *The Management of the Peterhof Museum Complex*

THE LOWER PARK

10. *The Great Cascade*
11. *The Samson Fountain*
12. *The Samson (Sea) Canal*
13. *The Voronikhin Colonnades*
14. *The Favourite Fountain*
15. *The Bowl (Italian) Fountain*
16. *The Bowl (French) Fountain*
17. *The Nymph Fountain*
18. *The Danaid Fountain*
19. *The Orangery Fountain*
20. *The Great Orangery*
21. *The Adam Fountain*
22. *The Sheaf, Cloche and Bench Trick Fountains*
23. *The Monplaisir Palace Museum*
24. *The Catherine Block Palace Museum*
25. *The Bathhouse Museum; the Chinese Garden*
26. *The Kitchen Block Museum*
27. *The Aviary Pavilions*
28. *The Sun Fountain*
29. *Monument to Peter the Great*
30. *The Oak Trick Fountain*
31. *The Umbrella Trick Fountain*
32. *The Fir Trick Fountain*
33. *The Roman Fountains*
34. *The Chessboard Hill Cascade*
35. *The Pyramid Fountain*
36. *The Museum of Wax Effigies*
37. *The Peterhof Landing Stage*
38. *The Whale Fountain; the Sand Pond*
39. *The Eve Fountain*
40. *The Illumination Yard restaurant*
41. *The Hermitage Pavilion*
42. *The Lion Cascade*
43. *The Marly Palace Museum*
44. *The Cloche (Triton) Fountains*
45. *The Golden Hill Cascade*
46. *The Ménagères (Economical) Fountains*
47. *The Venus Garden. The Marly Rampart*
48. *The Sectorial Ponds*
49. *The Juniper Bed*
50. *Old Peterhof, the territory of the Merchants' Harbour*
51. *Entrance to the Lower Park*

52. *The Benois Family Museum*
53. *The Publishing Department of the Peterhof State Museum-Reserve*
54. *Parking of excursion buses*
55. *Excursion Bureau*

T *Toilets*

P *Car parking*

THE UPPER GARDENS

The Upper Gardens. Pylons of the main gate.
Architect B. F. Rastrelli. 1754

C. Kaestner. Catherine the Great Leaving Peterhof. 1762

Here, at the entrance to the Upper Gardens, Alexei Orlov waited for Catherine
so as to accompany her to St Petersburg and proclaim the Empress of Russia

To the south the Great Peterhof Palace lies the Upper Park or Gardens 15 hectares in area. The territory of the gardens stretches between the façade of the palace and St Petersburg Highway. Its main entrance is marked by superb pylons. The layout of the Upper Gardens is well articulated with the palace – the green lawns and the fountain pools of the wide central parterre enable one to see the palace in all its grandeur from the very entrance. The clipped trees and bushes, covered avenues or *pergolas*, pavilions, marble and bronze statues – all these features were characteristic attributes of regular palatial gardens in the first half of the eighteenth century. The Upper Gardens played the role of the state courtyard or *cour d'honneur* of the Great Palace.

On Braunstein's 1716 draft the Upper Gardens are rectangular in plan, with a parterre on the north-south axis having the width equal to that of the façade of the Upper Chambers. It is worth mentioning that in the first quarter of the eighteenth century this part of the royal residence was known as a "kitchen garden".

Vegetables and greens were grown in beds there and three large ponds, which served as reservoirs of water for the fountain system of the Great Cascade, were also used to keep live fish. It was only in the second half of the eighteenth century that Peter's "kitchen-garden", as the area was called, was refashioned into a regular park. By that time the Great Palace had been built and its main entrance overlooked the road to St Petersburg instead of the terrace as was the case with the Upper Mansion. The beds and tiny gardens were ousted by avenues of skilfully trimmed trees and shrubs and with an introduction of trellised arbours and pergolas this small area began to look as a genuine formal garden.

*The Armorial Block of
the Great Peterhof Palace*

The construction of a tall railing that encircled the area of the Upper Gardens to a design by Francesco Bartolomeo Rastrelli on three sides in 1755–59 promoted the further development of the territory as an artistically integral complex. But the most important factor in this wondrous transformation was the construction of fountains. Three extensive pools with decorative structures known as the Mezheumny, Neptune's Chariot and Oak Fountains were added to the two Square Pools dug out in Peter's times. In this way the five-fountain composition was shaped in the Upper Gardens. After changing its decor several times over the past centuries, it has survived to the present day.

THE FOUNTAINS
OF THE SQUARE POOLS

The square pools are the oldest water reservoirs in the Upper Gardens. The digging of ponds began as early as 1719 according to a design by Jean-Baptiste Le Blond to the right and left of Peter's Upper Mansion. They were used for accumulating water necessary for the operation of the fountain system of the Lower Park. In 1773 the centre of each pool was decorated with sculptural groups on round platforms faced with tufa and lead dolphins spurting out water were placed around them. In the second half of the eighteenth century the worn-out sculptures were removed to be replaced with vertical water jets. In 1956, when the Upper Gardens were restored, the marble statue of *Venus Italica* was set up in the centre of the western pool and the figure of *Apollo* in its eastern counterpart.

Fountain of the Western Square
Pool and the Armorial Block
of the Great Peterhof Palace

A vast area at the other end of the axis of the Upper Gardens is occupied by a round pool adorned with four curved figures of dolphins at the sides and a fabulous sea monster in the centre, all spouting jets of water from their open jaws. The name of the fountain – the Mezheumny or Indefinite – reflects repeated changes to its sculptural decor. During the restoration of the fountain it was decided to take as a model for its decor the version known from a drawing in an eighteenth-century art book.

The round pool of the Oak Fountain lies on the central axis of the Upper Gardens, to the south of the square pools. The fountain owes its name to the oak tree cast in lead after a model by Carlo Bartolomeo Rastrelli and set up in the centre of the pool in 1734. Fifty years later it was shifted to the Lower Park. And only dolphins lying on the tufa mounds still continued to eject smoothly curving jets of water. In 1929 the figure of a putto by the Italian sculptor Giacomo de' Rossi in 1809 was installed in the centre of the pool.

The Upper Gardens. Sculpture: Zephyrus. 1757

The green parterre of the Upper Gardens is adorned with the marble figures by the Paduan sculptor Antonio Bonazza: Flora, the goddess of flowers, Zephyr, the warm Western wind, Vertumnus, the god of gardening, and his consort, Pomona, the goddess of fruit. The sculptor carved all the statues, remarkable for the rare excellence of execution, in 1757, as the inscriptions incised on their bases indicate. At the edge of the parterre, in front of the Great Palace, are small marble figures of Minerva, the goddess of wisdom, and Mercury, the god of trade

The Oak Fountain. Putto Putting on a Mask. Sculptor G. de' Rossi ▶

THE NEPTUNE FOUNTAIN AND
THE APOLLO CASCADE

In the centre of the Upper Gardens is a large rectangular pool. It runs along the main axis of the area and its smooth water surface blends with the green pieces of ground once intended for lawn bowling.

The pit used for the pool was dug out in 1721 as the main reservoir of water feeding the Great Cascade.

It was only in 1737 that the pool was decorated as a fountain – installed there was the sculptural group *Neptune's Chariot* made by Carlo Bartolomeo Rastrelli for Peter the Great as early as 1723. The elaborate composition of seventeen gilt lead sculptural pieces represented the sea god Neptune driving a chariot harnessed with four sea horses or *hippocampi*. Around them naiads and sirens were frolicking. The composition was completed by a copper-gilt ball raised high on a stream behind Neptune's back. Simultaneously with the setting up of *Neptune's Chariot* in 1737 at the southern side of the pool was created a small three-step cascade adorned with the gilt figure of *Winter* cast by Carlo Bartolomeo Rastrelli back in 1721.

In 1799 the former Neptune's Chariot used as a decoration of the central pool in the Upper Gardens was replaced with a beautiful sculptural group acquired in 1782 by Paul I, then the heir apparent, in

*Statue of Apollo Belvedere
and the Neptune Fountain*

24

The Neptune Fountain
Putto riding a sea dragon

The Neptune Fountain
Heraldic shields

The Neptune.
Warriop riding a hippocampus

Nuremberg. The newly installed piece of sculpture was designed by the two local masters, Christoph Ritter and Georg Schweigger. The figure of the sea god Neptune, crowned and holding a trident, stands on a high pedestal. Below are two nymphs on barrels symbolizing the Rivers Pegnitz and Rednitz which flow across Bavaria. The composition is enhanced by two warriors mounted on sea horses, hippocampi, and four putti riding dolphins and sea dragons. The pedestal features heraldic shields, masks and trumpeting putti.

Simultaneously with the setting up of Neptune's Chariot a small three-step cascade was constructed on the southern side of the pool in 1737. It was decorated with a lead figure of *Winter* cast by Carlo Bartolomeo Rastrelli earlier, in 1721. At the beginning of the nineteenth century it was replaced with the statue of *Apollo Belvedere* by the ancient Greek sculptor Leochares, cast in the workshop of the St Petersburg Academy of Arts. The cascade owes its new name to this sculpture.

◄ *The Neptune Fountain*

The Upper Gardens. View of the Great ►
Peterhof Palace from the Main Gate

The Mezheumny Fountain. Dragon

The Upper Gardens. Berceau

View the Great Peterhof Palace from the Mezheumny Fountain ▶

THE GREAT PALACE

*V. Sadovnikov. The Court Going Out
of the Great Peterhof Palace*

he Great Palace is the structural pivot of the ensemble uniting the Upper Gardens and the Lower Park. The axis of the garden parterre on the southern side and the straight line of the Sea Canal on the north are oriented towards its centre. The palace soars at the edge of a sixteen-metre-high natural terrace. The façade of the elegant three-storeyed building with its galleries and flanking wings – the Church and Armorial Blocks – stretches along the terrace for almost 300 metres. The Great Cascade serves as a majestic "pedestal" for the palace. The abundance of gold, the resplendent sculptural decor of the architecture, the pow-

erful motion and noise of the falling water, all creates a jubilant festive atmosphere.

The palace, however, did not look like we see it today from the very beginning and its role as the architectural focus of the grandiose ensemble was not determined at once. In 1714, when the laying out of the Sea Canal, the construction of the grotto and the cascade began according to Peter's concept, the building of the Upper Chambers having the winter and summer apartments started. Johann-Friedrich Braunstein was responsible for the initial architectural solution.

In keeping with the architectural laws predominant in Peter's age, the centre of the palace was given to an entrance hall and above it the hall with two tiers of windows was designed. A small staircase, still known as the state staircase, led to the hall. The apartments of the ground and first floors to the east and west of the hall were equipped as living rooms of the royal family and its guests. However, by that time it had been clear that neither the modest decoration nor the dimensions of the chambers corresponded to the major role attached to the building.

In 1716 Jean-Baptiste Le Blond, the new "Architect-General" possessing a truly outstanding artistic talent and large experience, immediately detected the lack of correspondence between the built chambers and the overall concept of the residence. Having taken measures to fix the loose walls with iron braces. Le Blond offered to Peter the Great his own design for the reconstruction and enlargement of the main interiors – the Hall, the State Stairway and the Study of Peter the Great. These plans were realized under the supervision of Braunstein after Le Blond's sudden death.

Vase on the roof of the Great Palace

Railing on the balcony of the Great Palace

In 1721 Michetti, who replaced Le Blond as Chief Architect, offered a new plan for the extension of the palace. One-storey galleries with wings giving a greater sweep to the Upper Chambers were built. However, this palace, stretching alongside the edge of the terrace for 160 metres, could meet the demands of the growing court only for a short time.

In 1747 Francesco Bartolomeo Rastrelli began, at the command of Empress Elizabeth Petrovna, a radical reconstruction of the Upper Chambers. He left intact only the central part of Peter's palace. Rastrelli enlarged the galleries and transformed the wings into the Church and Armorial Blocks. The wealth and dimensions of the apartments, which emerged thanks to the architect's brilliant talent and the skills of hundreds of first-rate craftsmen, produced a striking impression. The design of the royal residence fully conformed to the emotional and artistic task of creating a continuously unfolding pageant. The fact that the arrangement of the halls and rooms in the enfilade perfectly suited the idea of festive processions was confirmed not only during the famous *entrées* of the monarchs, but by all rites and even balls.

The luxurious gilt state staircase led to the no less richly adorned Ballroom and then to the new Anteroom also embellished with gilt carving and ceiling paintings. On passing it and turning to the door opposite it, guests found themselves on the axis of the state suite of the palace apartments. The suite seemed to be endless and the effect was further enhanced by a large window at the end of the perspective through which one's glance penetrated into the space of the park behind it.

Rastrelli's brilliant creations appeared during the last decade marked by the dominance of the Baroque style. The emergence of a new style, Classicism, which rapidly spread in Russia during the 1760s, called for new amendments in the interiors of the Great Palace.

Dome of
the Armorial Block

The Armorial Block ▶
of the Great Palace

The opulent and vast interiors, the superb mastery of the architect and hundreds of first-rate craftsmen produced an overwhelming impression. The disposition of halls and rooms in long enfilades was perfectly suitable for festive processions and ceremonies. The Main Staircase glittering with gold led to the luxurious Ballroom and further to the new Anteroom, also richly adorned with gilt carving and ceiling paintings. On passing it, guests found themselves on the axis of the enfilade of state rooms that seemed to be infinite. The impression was further enhanced by the window in the depth of the vista affording a view of the park.

Rastrelli's creations were produced in the last decade of the Baroque era and therefore many of them were doomed to have a short life. The new style, the new system of ideals that spread around Russia almost immediately in the 1760s, made the rulers engage in the alterations in the interiors of the Great Palace again.

In 1766–69 Jean-Baptiste Vallin de la Mothe made substantial alterations in the architectural decor of the palace's living apartments and state rooms, including the Dining-Room, the Great Hall and the Anteroom. During the subsequent 65 years the decor of the halls and rooms of the Great Peterhof Palace remained largely unaltered. And only in 1845 Andrei Stakenschneider added the second floor over the eastern wing of the palace and carried out repair work in the interiors.

E. Meyer. View of the Church of the Great Peterhof Palace. 1842

N. Schilder. *Portrait of Emperor Nicholas II*.
Late 19th century

E. Hau. The Church of SS Peter and Paul in the Great Peterhof Palace ▶

The court journals dating from that period and memories of contemporaries have retained their descriptions. For instance, the jeweller Jérémie Pausier active in Russia in the middle of the eighteenth century recalled: "The ladies of lower ranks usually wear brilliants costing ten to twelve thousand roubles. And I think that there is hardly any one possessing more precious decorations than the Russian Empress even among the sovereigns of entire Europe."

The 200-year-long history of the activities of outstanding architects and decorators at Peterhof turned the Great Palace into an outstanding cultural memorial that concentrated a great number of superb works of painting, sculpture, furniture, bronze, porcelain and glass ware. In the Soviet period the Great Palace, the former major imperial country residence, was converted into a museum.

The court journals dating from that period and memories of contemporaries have retained their descriptions. For instance, the jeweller Jérémie Pausier active in Russia in the middle of the eighteenth century recalled: "The ladies of lower ranks usually wear brilliants costing ten to twelve thousand roubles. And I think that there is hardly any one possessing more precious decorations than the Russian Empress even among the sovereigns of entire Europe."

Detail of painted decoration of the Main Staircase with the state emblem of the Russian Empire

Today, in the same way as during the reign of Elizabeth Petrovna, the entrance to the palace is on the side of the Upper Gardens. The galleries of the ground floor lead to the western wing, to a spacious vestibule with marble floor and further to the Main Staircase. The streams of light, the rich colours of the painting and the glamour of gold produce an indelible impression. The stairwell rises through all the three stories. Its marches are running along the walls, and the immense height of the interior is evident from the first step. The walls are covered with painted decoration imitating relief floral garlands, vase and mythological creatures placed in painted semicircular niches. These illusory niches correspond to the real ones, embellished with carved ornaments and gilt wooden figures of *Autumn* and *Winter*. Two companion statues, *Summer* and *Spring*, stand opposite these figures. The vases painted on the walls echo the unusually whimsical carved vases on the newels of the staircase banisters. The light pouring in from the real windows is reflected in the mirrors imitating windows on the opposite walls. The walls smoothly turn through the painted coves into the ceiling entirely covered with an allegoric painting by the Venetian artist Bartolomeo Tarsia featuring Empress Elizabeth in the guise of Spring. The magnificence of the interior is enhanced by the inlaid parquet floors and the wrought-iron grille with gilt details.

The artistic decor of the Main Staircase includes the images of the seasons and times of day, the elements, etc., which are characteristic of the Baroque. Similarly to the plafond, the two allegorical figures *Loyalty* and *Justice* over the portal of the door leading to the Ballroom extol the monarchy, as do numerous double-headed eagles, crowns and monograms E I recalling Empress Elizabeth Petrovna.

The restorers carefully preserved the surviving fragments of the old wall painting and returned the rescued figure of *Winter* and a vase to their original places.

Sculpture: Spring

G. Valeriani.
The Rape of Europa

THE BALLROOM

The room stretches along the south–north axis and occupies the entire western wing of the palace, 270 square metres in area. The Ballroom is one of the most luxurious halls designed by Rastrelli. The abundance of windows and mirrors between them, all framed by elaborate gilt carvings, create an illusion of a vast space thanks to their repeated reflections in the mirrored "windows" on the opposite wall. This illumination of the hall by the gilt sconces, seemingly growing out of the luxurious frame mounts, enhances this feeling.

The impression of a vast expanse and great height is emphasized by the painted coving that seems to break the surface of the ceiling and a giant painted ceiling painting, *Parnassus*, executed by Bartolomeo Tarsia in 1751. The ceiling painting continues to glorify Empress Elizabeth Petrovna as a patroness of the arts in Russia.

In addition to the paintings of the cove and ceiling, the architect placed over the mirrors 16 tondos by the Italian artist Giuseppe Valeriani painted with subjects borrowed from *Metamorphoses* by Ovid and *Aeneid* by Virgil. The inlaid parquet floor with a pattern in the form of large stars adds to the colour gamut of the hall decoration. From the time of its creation the Ballroom was used for festive receptions, dinners and balls. In the early twentieth century some meetings of state importance took place here. It was in this room that the State Duma was proclaimed by the special Peterhof meeting in 1905.

Behind the Baroque Ballroom is the former Anteroom designed by Rastrelli which owes its name to the position in front of the main hall of the Great Palace – the Throne Room. In this room the officials who came for a reception used to wait for the beginning of the ceremony.

The architect placed the Anteroom in the north-western corner having oriented one of its windows onto the axis of the suite of state rooms which was also completed by a window at its other end. The decor of this interior– the gilt wooden carving adorning the walls, the gilt sconces and the painted ceiling – was similar to the Ballroom.

In the 1770s Yury Velten decorated the Anteroom in a different style by orders of Catherine the Great. He replaced the gilt carving of the walls by moulded plaster details and bas-reliefs, but retained Rastrelli's parquet floor and the ceiling painting *Ceres, the Goddess of Fecundity, Handing Over the Ears of Corn to the First Ploughman Triptolemus* by Laurent Werner. The main embellishment of the hall became the twelve huge canvases painted in 1771–72 by the German painter Jacob Philippe Hackaert on the Empress's instruction. The paintings cover almost the entire surface of the walls in two tiers. They feature various episodes of the expeditions of the Russian fleet to the Archipelago – the islands of the Aegean Sea, Asia Minor and the Balkan Coastland – that played an important role in the course of the Russo-

*J. Ph. Hackaert. The Burning of the Turkish Fleet
in the Chesme Harbour. 1772*

Turkish War of 1768–74, the battles of the Russian fleet
against the Turks and especially the crucial battle in the
Chesme harbour on 26 June 1770that proved to be victorious for the Russians.

Contemporaries mentioned a curious detail that had
preceded the painting of the canvas. In order to give the
artist an opportunity to depict the sea battle in a more re-
alistic manner, the Empress ordered to blow up a frigate
on the roadstead of the Italian port of Livorno where the
Russian squadron was stationed. This fact struck Europeans. The Chesme Hall, as the interior came to be called after this period, became a sort of artistic monument to Russia's naval glory, particularly befitting Peterhof that was
created by the founder of the Russian navy.

*A. Terwesten. The Sacrifice of Iphigenia.
Detail of ceiling painting*

J. Ph. Hackaert. The Destruction of the Russian Ship "St Eustaphius". 1771

J. Ph. Hackaert. The Burning of the Turkish Fleet in the Mitilena Harbour on 2 November 1771. 1773

Bust of Alexei Orlov. Sculptor G. Cibei. 1770s

During the expeditions to the Archipelago Catherine the Great appointed Alexei Orlov the Commander-in-Chief of the Russian Fleet and it was he who accepted the paintings featuring the scenes of the Russo-Turkish War from Jacob Philippe Hackaert

51

At the beginning of the war canvases by Hackaert were evacuated. But the plafond painting by the Italian painter Laurent Werner, which had once adorned the ceiling, perished in fire. Now the painting produced by the German artist Augustin Terwesten in 1690 occupies its place on the ceiling. It features a scene from the history of the legendary Trojan War. The action is set in the Aegean Sea – the same place where the Battle of Chesme took place. The Greek King Agamemnon who enraged the goddess Artemis, vowed to sacrifice his daughter Iphigenia to the goddess. Augustin Terwesten depicted the moment of the sacrifice when the goddess substitutes Iphigenia for a doe on the altar and carries Iphigenia to Tauris to turn the young girl into her priestess.

J. Ph. Hackaert. The Battle near the City of Patras. Episode of the First Expedition of the Russian Fleet to the Archipelago. 1773

he room adjoining the Chesme Hall seems to be small in comparison with the vast state rooms. Its windows afford views of the Lower and Upper Parks and large glazed French windows lead to the gallery linking it with the Armorial Block, which once was occupied by the private apartments of Catherine the Great and now houses a display of the Special Treasury.

In the middle of the eighteenth century the room was decorated according to a design by Rastrelli – the wooden panels were

54

V. Sadovnikov. The Court Leaving the Great Palace at Peterhof. Mid-19th century

embellished with gilt carving and the walls lined with blue silk, hence its name. In the past the Blue Reception Room had an auxiliary character. It was used by the secretaries and household officials, who made records day after day about court life in the palace in special journals. So a desk with a writing set occupies the central place in the display of this interior.

Deserving special mention among the paintings decorating the walls of the Blue Reception Room is the canvas on the western wall depicting the Great Palace and the Great Cascade. It was painted by the famous Russian seascape painter Ivan Aivazovsky in 1837. The exhibition allows one of to form an idea of the decor of official palatial rooms.

Vase. The Imperial Porcelain Factory, St Petersburg. Ca 1830

he Throne Room, occupying an area of 330 square metres, is the largest interior in the palace's suite of state rooms. The snow-white ceiling with a high coving and lavish stucco decoration, the mirrors and chandeliers shimmering like amethyst, the bright red spots of the draperies on the windows and the upholstery of the throne, all contributes to a particularly festive and majestic air dominating the room.

In the past this room was known as the Large Hall. Its dimensions, streams of light from the twenty-eight windows arranged in two tiers, an abundance of gold, the huge painted ceiling by Bartolomeo Tarsia and the skilfully arranged pattern of its parquet floor were all intended to emphasize the significance of this interiors in the suite of magnificent apartments. During the Elizabethan period the hall was used for coronation ceremonies, large festive dinners and naturally for balls. Later official receptions began to be held here.

The change of artistic tastes and a new stylistic concept led to major alterations in the design of the room. In 1777–78 Yury Velten redesigned it in the then predominant Neo-Classical style. The plafond was replaced by a smooth ceiling with a moulded frame. The main accent in the decor of the room was placed on the eastern wall in front of which the throne was installed. Velten hung there a huge portrait of Catherine the Great painted by the Dutch artist Vigilius Erichsen in 1762. She is shown riding her favourite horse Brilliant, in the uniform of the colonel of the Preobrazhensky Regiment – at the moment when she, having just become the Empress, is returning from St Petersburg to Peterhof. Painted soon after the coup, the portrait became one of the principal highlights of the Peterhof Palace. Nowadays, against the background of the equestrian portrait of Catherine the Great, on a three-step dais, stands the throne armchair commissioned, according to legend, by Alexander Menshikov for receptions of Peter the Great in his palace.

To further enhance the significance of the eastern wall, Velten placed at the sides two round reliefs, *Justice and Truth* and *Virtue* by the sculptor Ivan Prokofyev. The bas-reliefs were executed in the 1770s. The overdoor portraits by Heinrich Buchholz featuring Elizabeth Petrovna, Anna Ioannovna and Catherine I appeared here by orders of Catherine the Great and were supposed to remind about a long tradition of women on the Russian throne.

An important role in the decorative scheme of the Throne Room, sometimes used for receptions of foreign embassies, were paintings illustrating the Battle of Chesme, for this naval victory was one of the most glorious episodes in the Russian history of the eighteenth century. The paintings were produced for the Russian court by the English painter Richard Paton in 1771–72.

The Throne. Russia.
Early 18th century

Footrest for the throne.
Russia. Mid-18th century

H. Buchholz. Portrait
of Empress Catherine I.
Last quarter of the 18th century

H. Buchholz.
Portrait of Empress
Anna Ioannovna.
Between 1770
and 1800

Clock: Apollo's Chariot.
France. Late 18th century

H. Buchholz.
Portrait of Empress
Elizabeth Petrovna.
Last quarter of the
18th century

Clock: Nymph and Cupid.
France. 18th century

his hall which received in the nineteenth century one more name, the Room of Ladies-in-Waiting, was not reconstructed by Velten and until 1941 retained the superb decor of the mid-eighteenth century.

Rastrelli introduced a large composite order into the decor of its walls with the pilasters functioning as a sort of framework. The piers between the pilasters were occupied by two tiers of windows, mirrors, huge doors and another kind of mirrors imitating windows. The walls were covered with a dynamic, fancifully intertwining carved and gilt ornament of plant shoots and rocaille motifs. Moving around the room one could notice that the mirrors set opposite to one another, reproduced new and new perspective views creating an illusion of an infinite space.

In 1753 the basic amount of work in the Audience Hall was completed. The artist Pietro Ballarini, who arrived from Italy, was entrusted to paint a plafond based on *Jerusalem Delivered*, the famous poem by Torquato Tasso devoted to the first Crusade. Ballarini chose a moment when the Christian knight Rinaldo implored the Saracen girl Armida not to kill herself but to become his wife.

J. G. Kirchner. St Wenceslaus.
The Royal Porcelain Factory,
Meissen. Ca 1730

The Audience Room from the very beginning was regarded as one of those rooms where official receptions were to be held. However, later, in the nineteenth century, the ceremonies began to take place in the adjacent Throne Room and the Audience Hall was given to the ladies-in-waiting. They stayed in this room during official dinners, when tables were laid simultaneously in all the state rooms of the palace.

Restored in 1979, the Audience Room. with its gilt decor reflected in the numerous mirrors, produces, as before, a magnificent impression. All the valuable museum exhibits sent to the rear of the country during the war – the majestic gilt sconces placed on the walls by orders of Catherine the Great in 1778, the clock with a musical mechanism, a work by the Paris clock-maker Giles the Elder, active in the second half of the eighteenth century, and many other objects – have returned to their original places.

Porcelain statuettes on a console table.
The Royal Porcelain Factory, Meissen.
Mid-18th century

After the luxury and glitter of the Audience Hall the White Dining-Room located in the suite of state rooms evokes a sense of unusual calm and harmony. Bright tones are dominant in the decor of this interior devoid of painting. Only the parquet floor with a zigzag pattern reminds of Rastrelli's original decoration.

In 1774–75 Yury Velten completely altered the interior and fashioned it in the style of Classicism, which had ousted the fanciful Baroque decor. On the huge smooth panels partitioning the wall, he placed several decorations in high-relief: trophies of hunting and fishing, gardening tools, etc. Like in some earlier interiors, the architect made use of ancient mythological subjects here – the room features scenes from a myth about the love between Dionysus, the god of wine, and Ariadne. The room has a particularly majestic appearance owing to two stoves faced by single-tone tiles with classical reliefs, also produced after a design by Velten.

Items of the Husk Service.
The Etruria potteries
of Josiah Wedgwood,
Staffordshire, England.
18th century

The interior had been called the Large Dining-Room, but from the middle of the nineteenth century it became known under a different name, the White Dining-Room. It was used for official dinners held in a majestic and luxurious atmosphere. The dinner service, now on display in the White Dining-Room, was for a long time used for such dinners. The set is a fine example of "Queen Ware" produced for Catherine the Great at the Etruria potteries in England under the supervision of Josiah Wedgwood, one of the most famous ceramists of Europe. Today 196 pieces from this service are kept at Peterhof. The glass objects displayed on the table were made in Russia and Bohemia in the eighteenth century.

The Dining-Room is illuminated by five luxurious chandeliers, the ormolu frames of which are embellished with bluish-lilac crystal pendants shaped like oak leaves. One of these chandeliers was the largest in the Russian palaces. All of them, like the girandoles standing on the table and near the windows, were manufactured at the St Petersburg Glass Works in the 1760s and 1770s.

Bust of Empress Catherine the Great.
Sculptor G. Cibei. 1770s

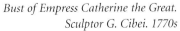

The Western and Eastern Chinese Lobbies, a tribute to the infatuation with Oriental art, are located symmetrically to the central axis of the Great Palace. They occupy small rooms of Peter's Upper Mansion and were adorned in 1766–79 after designs by Jean-Baptiste Vallin de la Mothe, who used for facing the walls of these rooms authentic Chinese lacquered screens brought to Russia during the age of Peter the Great. The screens are painted with traditional Chinese subjects: landscapes with islands and bridges, people engaged in everyday occupations, etc. The lower parts of the walls, the window reveals, the doors and, at last, the ceilings are painted "in a Chinese taste" by the Russian master craftsman Fiodor Vlasov and his assistants.

The rich decor of the lobbies – lacquered panels on the walls, the ceilings painted in imitation of porcelain, the striking figure-shaped floors inlaid of tiny bits of valuable kinds of wood, ceramic stoves unparalleled in the Russian palaces due to their elaborate outlines – was to conjure up in the viewer the exotic realm of distant Oriental countries. Such lobbies were intended for keeping collections of decorative and applied art, mainly of Chinese and Japanese wares. However, the chinoiserie for such specific "kunstkammers" were bought in European countries as well, which did not evade a general fascination with the Orient.

Today the Chinese Lobbies of the Great Palace house the largest collections of Japanese and Chinese porcelain, vividly coloured enamels from Canton and lacquered caskets from Beijing. Of particular interest among the furniture items are a writing desk of Chinese work, chairs with lacquer decoration executed by English cabinet-makers of the eighteenth century (the Eastern Lobby) and the French cylinder bureau decorated with Chinese lacquer insets (the Western Lobby).

The Western Chinese Lobby

67

The Western Chinese Lobby.
Candlesticks of Chinese porcelain
and a clock

The Western Chinese
Lobby. Incence-burner
in the shape of duck.
China. Late 17th –
early 18th century

The Western Chinese Lobby.
Dog Fo (the Buddha's dog)

68

The Eastern Chinese Lobby

The Eastern Chinese Lobby.
Chinese Man and Chinese Woman.
By J. Kändler. The Meissen Porcelain
Factory. Germany. Ca 1760

The Eastern Chinese Lobby.
Cockerel. China
18th century

The Eastern Chinese Study.
Desk. China.
First half of the 18th century

The Eastern Chinese
Lobby. Pheasants.
China. 18th century

View of the northern suite ▶
from the Western Chinese Lobby

*T*n the centre of the earliest part of the palace lies a hall with two tiers of windows that stretches from its northern to southern wall. Its windows overlook the parterre of the Upper Gardens and the Great Cascade with the Sea Canal and fountains in the Lower Park. Therefore this hall is the focal point of the layout of the immense palace and park ensemble, and its location across the suite direction enhances even more the interior's link with the layout of the park space. The hall has a special air of magnificence about it not only due to the two rows of windows, but also because of its location at the juncture of the two principal axes of the park. Moreover, it produces a formidable impression thanks to the wealth and variety of its decorative elements – the painted ceiling glorifying Peter the Great and the multicoloured cove with its medallions featuring the ancient deities Cybele, Juno, Hefaestos and Neptune as symbols the four elements, the patron of the arts Apollo and the allegories of war – Mars and Bellona. The beautiful snow-white frieze running along the perimeter of the hall under the cove contains rectangular reliefs with the attributes of the arts, sciences, symbols of naval victories and trophies of war alternating with paired consoles representing seasons of the year. And last, the hall is embellished with luxuriant gilt carvings, mirrors and numerous portraits of young girls looking at visitors from the walls.

It was the principal and largest interior in Peter's Upper Mansion known commonly just as the Hall. The Hall, 110 square metres in area, was first decorated after a design by Jean-Baptiste Le Blond and later by Niccolo Michetti. However, the architects' concepts were fully realized only after the death of Peter the Great, in 1726. In those times the hall was provided with fireplaces arranged opposite one another, with mirrors over them, at the western and eastern walls. The decor of the Hall consisted of the

73

moulded compositions symbolizing the arts, sciences, military activities and navigation, as well as the oak panels running along the lower part of the walls, and the four tapestries. In 1723 the Italian painter Bartolomeo Tarsia offered to Peter the Great to decorate the Hall with a ceiling painting conveying the idea of the flowering of the Fatherland under a powerful and wise monarch. A contract with the painter was signed only in 1726 and already in August that year the painted plafond by Tarsia, the earliest at Peterhof, adorned the ceiling.

During the reconstruction of the palace in the middle of the eighteenth century Francesco Bartolomeo Rastrelli decorated the panels, doors and window reveals by a fanciful gilt carved pattern (the work was executed by Russian carvers). In 1764 the Hall changed its appearance again. Jean-Baptiste Vallin de La Mothe arranged on the walls of the Hall in the so-called "tapestry-like" manner, or from top to bottom, 368 paintings acquired by orders of Catherine the Great from the widow of the Italian artist Pietro Rotari who had died in St Petersburg. Most of them are represen-

P. Rotari. Girl with a Book.
Mid-18th century

Fireplace trivet:
Vulcan

tations of young models in variety of costumes painted both by the artist himself and his pupils. Some works are based on genre and mythological subjects and some others are skillfully made trompe-l'oeil pieces. After this acquisition the room came to be called the Picture or Portrait Hall or the Hall of Fashions and Graces.

In the 1840s, the architect Andrei Stakenschneider made minor changes in the decoration of the Hall. After the reconstruction of the Hall, destroyed during the War of 1941–45, all the 368 paintings were returned to it. The mantelpieces were adorned with eighteenth-century French bronze clocks and surviving Meissen porcelain figurines. Veritable masterpieces of French bronzework are the pair of trivets representing Venus and Vulcan.

The rooms following the Eastern Chinese Lobby are typical for eighteenth-century palaces and as a rule formed the complex of female apartments – a boudoir, a bedroom, a dressing room and a study.

The first of them, is the Boudoir, or the Partridge Drawing-Room, situated near the Bedroom and intended for conversations in an intimate circle. The room, located in a jutty, has three windows and a wooden partition with a recess on the southern side. Rastrelli designed this interior instead of two rooms of Peter's mansion. The architect also placed in the semicircular niche a settee, richly carved in a Baroque vein and with its walls curving smoothly alongside the room's wall. In 1771, however, Yury Velten built by orders of Catherine the Great a new partition completely changing the design of the room, but the niche with a sofa was left untouched.

It is largely to the silk lining of its walls that the room owes its especially ornate look. Wreathes, garlands, ears of ripe corn and leaves scattered on a blue ground form a sort of a garden trellis through which the sky is visible. Groups of partridges scurrying amidst tufts of tall grass and flowers recur in a definite rhythm against this background. This pictorial motif gave to the Boudoir its second name, which perfectly suited the designation of the room used as an intimate interior.

The silk pattern was designed by the brilliant French draughtsman Philippe de La Salle and the fabric was produced around 1770 in Lyons, a famous centre of French silk-making, under the artist's supervision. However, the original French silk has not survived to this day. The worn-out fabrics were periodically replaced by identical ones. Before the War of 1941–45 the walls of the drawing-room were lined with silk reproduced at the Moscow Factory of the Sapozhnikov Brothers in 1897. The reserve roll of this fabric, evacuated to the rear of the country during the war, became a sample for the creation of new silk and was also enough to upholster one of the walls in the room.

J.-B. Greuze.
Girl Sitting by the Table. 1760s

The Partridge Drawing-Room was adorned in the past with portraits of the girls, the first graduates (in 1776) of the Smolny Institute for Noble Girls established by Catherine the Great. The portraits were painted by the eminent Russian painter Dmitry Levitsky. At the beginning of the twentieth century the portraits were transferred to the Russian Museum. On the eastern wall hangs a copy of the portrait of Yekaterina Nelidova, painted in the nineteenth century by Heinrich Schmidt, as a reminder about the former decoration of the Boudoir. The paintings of girls' heads by the well-known French artist Jean-Baptiste Greuze adorn the opposite wall. The harp standing in the centre was made in the London workshop of Sebastian Erard, a noted designer of musical instruments.

Fan. France. 1760s

P. Rotari.
*Portrait of Grand Duchess
Yekaterina Alexeyevna*

H. Schmidt.
Portrait of
Yekaterina Nelidova

he State Bedroom, which began to be called the Divan Room in the second half of the eighteenth century, is situated in the north-western jutty of the palace's central section. Thanks to the additional third window on the side eastern wall the room has more light. Like the Partridge Drawing-Room, it is adorned with carved and gilt wooden panels and fabrics on the walls. The southern wall is a wooden partition with an alcove decorated by an elegantly traced gilt ornament and two sculptural pairs of frolicking putti, looking out playfully from the door apertures by the alcove. Thus a complex of two bedchambers – the Empress's Bedroom and the Crown Bedroom, similar to it in decor – was created. Originally, a state bedstead stood in the alcove, but later a large Turkish divan was installed in this room, hence its name. Tradition has it that the divan was presented to Catherine the Great by her favourite Grigory Potemkin. In the same period, in 1779, a "Turkish partition" or a screen in the Gothic style designed by Yury Velten was installed. It cut the suite off the main volume of the room. Soon the wall dividing the niche on the southern side in two parts was destroyed and the Divan and the Crown Rooms were thus joined to form a single interior. Catherine the Great rarely used the Divan Room as a bedchamber – a room was fitted out for this purpose in the Armorial Block.

The walls of the Divan Room are upholstered in silk with a fine watercolour pattern – a "Chinese fabric with various figures", as recorded in documents. Such silk was produced in China in the seventeenth

Clock. France. 1760s

and eighteenth centuries. The watercolour decorations featured usual everyday scenes: fishing, hunting, tea-drinking, conversations in a garden, etc. During the Second World War the valuable silk was evacuated, but it was then already in a dangerous state. After the war the silk was restored and embellished the Divan Room again, but it is in need of new restoration now. Therefore it was decided to produce copies for wall hanging and to keep the authentic silk in the museum's stocks.

Visitors often pay attention to large feather pillows in satin cases lying on the immense "Turkish" sofa and similar coverlets finely embroidered in satin-stitch. This work was done in 1889 by craftsmen at the F. Korovin Factory in Moscow according to the old specimens with "Chinese patterns" to replace the worn-out authentic Chinese silks.

Of particular interest among objects kept in the room for a long time are a portrait of Elizabeth Petrovna as a child, an eighteenth-century copy by Heinrich Buchholz from the work by Louis Caravaque; the porcelain egg-shaped vase made at the Imperial Porcelain Factory in the middle of the eighteenth century; and a strikingly perfect porcelain sculpture featuring Catherine's pet Zemira, an Italian greyhound, lying on a pillow. The figurine of the greyhound was produced at the Imperial Porcelain Factory in 1779 after a model by Jean Dominique Rachette.

Porcelain sculpture: Zemira.
After the model by
J. D. Rachette

The Divan Room. Vase. By I. G. Miller.
The Imperial Porcelain Factory,
St Petersburg, Russia. After 1756

Painted silk. China. 18th century

H. Buchholz.
Portrait of Elizabeth Petrovna
as a Child. Mid-18th century

THE DRESSING ROOM

his room, retaining Rastrelli's decor, was absolutely identical to the Study both in size and finish and did not alter its appearance until the War of 1941–45. The silk, however, was replaced many times, and in 1845, for example, "white silk with coloured bouquets" was hung in the room. Nowadays it is adorned with a fine silk woven at the Factory of the Sapozhnikov Brothers for the Eastern Wing of the Great Palace as early as the middle of the nineteenth century.

The present-day display of the Dressing Room is an almost exact replica of the exhibition that existed before the war. Like before, a "toilet set of pink porcelain with gilding and flowers" stands on a dressing table. It was delivered to the palace from the Imperial Porcelain Factory in 1838. A fashion for the so-called "pink porcelain" lasted for many years. Besides the toilet set, a whole fireplace with a mirror frame, candelabra and clocks was brought to the Peterhof palace in 1849. The fireplace was destoryed during the war, while the clocks and candelabra adorn the Dressing Room to this day.

Over the dressing table hangs the formal portrait of Empress Elizabeth Petrovna painted one year before her death, in 1760, by the court painter Carle Vanloo, an eminent French artist. One more portrait of the Empress can be seen on the opposite wall. This is the authorial replica of the portrait of Georg Christophor Grooth showing Elizabeth with a black boy. The Empress liked the picture and it enjoyed success not in Russia alone. The composition of the portrait was reproduced at the Meissen Porcelain Factory in Germany.

*Unknown painter.
Portrait of Empress Catherine II.
18th century*

*Unknown Russian artist. Portrait
of Emperor Peter III. Last quarter
of the 18th century*

Toilet set. The Imperial Porcelain Factory,
St Petersburg. 1838

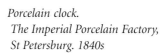

Porcelain clock.
The Imperial Porcelain Factory,
St Petersburg. 1840s

C. Vanloo. Portrait of Empress ▶
Elizabeth Petrovna. 1760

he name of this room did not imply that its owner was regularly engaged in state affairs in this interior. She would drop in quite often just to play a game of cards in a narrow circle of close associates. But the Study's furnishings were supposed to emphasize the seriousness of her occupations. Admittedly, the trimming of this room was not much different from the decor of the adjacent interiors – the same silks lining the walls and carved and gilt decoration on the doors and panels. In the middle of the nineteenth century the Study was embellished with a luxurious porcelain fireplace, with its set including a porcelain table and a screen. All these objects perished in the fire of 1941. Now a splendid white satin with flower basket motifs decorates the walls of the room. Precisely the same kind of silk hung on the walls throughout the nineteenth century. Its origins are probably traceable to the French silk manufactured at Lyons in the 1760s or 1770s and later copied at Russian factories.

A desk with numerous drawers and a superstructure in the centre of the room serves to stress that this room is a study. However, a large number of "knick-knacks" – candelabra, small vases, clocks, etc. – can be observed in the room. Deserving special attention among them is an ormolu clock shaped like a lyre mounted on a pedestal of white marble. The clock was made by the French clockmaker Jean Simon Bourdier in the 1770s or 1780s.

The Study is one of a few interiors in the palace where the furniture of several celebrated cabinet-makers has been collected. One of them is Georges Jacob – a famous French master active in the second half of the eighteenth century. He worked in the Classicist style and found most precise proportions and expressive silhouettes for items intended for seating. The fine gilt furniture set adorning the Study confirms his great renown. No less famous was the German cabinet-maker David Roentgen. Catherine the Great commissioned him to make the most valuable pieces for her collection. Worthy of particular interest are the portraits of Catherine the Great by Vigilius Erichsen and a portrait of Elizabeth Petrovna by an unknown Russian painter of the eighteenth century. On the eastern wall hangs the canvas Neptune's Grotto at Tivoli by the well-known German artist Jacob Philippe Hackaert, who permanently resided in Italy.

J. P. Hackaert. Neptune's Grotto at Tivoli.
Late 18th century

The Empress's Study. Twin vases with
the figures of naiads. Designed by
A. Voronikhin. The Imperial Porcelain
Factory, St Petersburg, Russia. 1800s

*V. Erichsen.
Portrait of Catherine
the Great*

*Clock shaped as a lyre.
By J. S. Bourdier.
France. 18th century*

*Unknown 19th-century
Russian painter.
Portrait of Emperor Paul I*

THE PASSAGE
OR STANDARD ROOM

In the earlier palace inventories this room has two names – more often it is called the Passage Room, but from the second half of the nineteenth century onwards another name, the Standard Room, appears. The latter is explained by a tradition to keep in it the standards of the Guards Regiment quartered at Peterhof in the summer season. For some time the walls of the room were lined with a yellow fabric, which corresponded to the colour of the imperial standard. However, the more customary name, Passage Room, is more in keeping with the function of the room located, as it was, right in front of the private apartments. The fabrics on the walls were replaced several times, as was usually the case. During the postwar restoration silk for lining the walls were hung with the silk woven after the surviving example of the 1840s produced specially for the Peterhof Palace at the Ivan Kondrashev Factory near Moscow.

Like in other rooms of the suite, the paintings in the Standard Room continue the gallery of formal portraits. The most interesting among them is

a work by an Italian artist Jacopo Amigoni, which represents Peter the Great with Minerva, the goddess of wisdom and patroness of fertility and peaceful labour.

Of greatest value among the furniture items of the Passage Room are the two rare pieces. One is a small commode with three drawers, which stands near the western wall. It bears the hallmark of Bernard van Risenburg, a major ebenist of the mid-eighteenth century. Another interesting item is a gaming table adorned in the marquetry technique by the Russian craftsman Nikolai Vasilyev in the 1770s. This table, recorded in all early inventories of the palace's property, bears on its top and under it finely executed representations of architectural structures, landscapes and the composition *The Arcadian Shepherds*.

Unknown Russian painter. Portrait
of Empress Catherine the Great.
Second half of the 18th century

Details of a gaming table.
By N. Vasilyev. Russia. 1770s

J. Amigoni.
Portrait of Peter
the Great
with Minerva

THE ROOM FOR
CAVALIERS-IN-ATTENDANCE

The name of the room is connected with the custom allowing the court cavaliers-in-attendance and upper ranks of the Guard officers to show an honour to Her Majesty by kissing her hand. In the eighteenth century, from the reign of Catherine the Great onwards, the Cavalier Guards used to stand on duty by Her Majesty's private apartments. The Empress had her own special interest in being not indifferent to the Guards, who played an immense role in her coming to the throne.

The walls of the room are hung with crimson brocade woven after the surviving pre-war specimen used to upholster the walls in 1898 instead of the worn-out earlier fabric. It was made at the F. Korovin Silk Factory in Moscow. Like all the rooms in the northern state suite of the palace, the Room for Cavaliers-in-Attendance was lavishly adorned by Rastrelli with gilt and carved rocaille motifs and female masks. A special role was attached to the door surrounds

showing an amazing fantasy in its design of the whimsically meandering shoots and leaves of plants. The sumptuous decorations over the doors consisting of female heads and flanking birds with opened or folded wings, created an impression of a fabulous richness. That is why the northern suite had another title, the Golden Suite.

According to the palace's inventories, the furniture decoration of the room was altered several times in the course of the eighteenth and nineteenth centuries in keeping with the prevalent fashions and even more often to meet the tastes and whims of the crowned owner. Deserving special interest among the paintings created in the second half of the seventeenth century are the *Horrors of War*, a canvas from the workshop of Peter Paul Rubens, *The Battle of the French and Flemings* painted by Adam Frans van der Meulen, court painter to Louis XIV, and *Cavalry Battle* by Jacques Courtois called Le Bourguignon.

One of Rastrelli's plans shows a small room with a single window. Later, to increase the size of the adjacent interior, the Room for Cavaliers-in-Attendance, this room was united with it. After the war the two rooms were recreated according to the original version. Thus the Small Passage Room was formed.

The Small Passage Room fascinates by the strikingly beautiful design and succulent colours of the silk lining its walls. This is the authentic mid-nineteenth century fabric produced specially for Peterhof at the G. Sapozhnikov Factory in Moscow. There are two remarkable portraits by Italian artists in this room – *Portrait of the Italian Poetess Vittoria Accoramboni*, whose life story is described in Stendhal's *Italian Chronicles*, by the sixteenth-century painter Scipione Pulzone, and *Portrait of an Old Man in an Oriental Dress* by Giandomenico Tiepolo.

The Small Passage Room. S. Pulzone.
Portrait of the Italian Poetess
Vittoria Accoramboni. 1570s

The Room for
Cavaliers-in-Attendance.
The Rubens school.
Horrors of War

97

THE LARGE
BLUE DRAWING-ROOM

his large room with three windows on the northern façade opens the suite of state interiors running through the entire Great Palace from west to east. According to Rastrelli's project, the hall located at the junction of the basic part of the building and the Eastern Wing with its living apartments, was to be employed, when necessary, as a dining-room for intimate family dinners or small banquets.

The walls, now adorned with carved and gilt panels, were originally upholstered with a pink fabric. The ceiling was decorated with a plafond painted by Laurent Werner. The coves were adorned with cartouches containing the monogram of Elizabeth Petrovna encircled by depictions of war trophies and garlands of flowers. A major item of decoration was also the high stove in the south-eastern corner faced with "landscape" tiles. Later, in the 1770s, a marble fireplace with a huge mirror appeared in the western wall.

L. E. Vigée-Lebrun.
Portrait of Empress
Maria Fiodorovna. 1800s

The room's special position among the living apartments was emphasized by its large height. Silk on the walls of the room was replaced several times, until the middle of the nineteenth century, when they were hung with a light-blue brocatelle, which gave to the room its alternative name, the Blue Drawing-Room. In the second half of the nineteenth century the plafond was replaced by a painted rosette styled in imitation of the rocaille motif of the cove. In 1848 a fine porcelain chandelier for 86 lights made at the Imperial Porcelain Factory embellished the room.

Between 1849 and 1853, the same factory made specially for the Great Palace a huge dinner service, part of which is now displayed on the tables in the room. The service, intended for 250 diners and consisting of more than 5,500 items, was used for festive receptions and banquets, and so the room began to be called the Banqueting Hall. The room derives its second name, the Cabbage-Leaf Service, from the service with such pictorial motif produced at the famous Sèvres Factory in the 1760s and used as a model for the Peterhof set. The variety of forms of the Banqueting Service and its subtle floral design attest to the high skills of the factory's craftsmen. Some of the items are placed in magnificent ebony cupboards with ormolu reliefs and sculptural decorations marked by brilliant modelling and fine finish. The bases of the pilasters bear the inscription of Ferdinande Barbedienne, a well-known bronzesmith of the mid-nineteenth century.

In addition to the majestic furnishings of the Blue Drawing-Room, its walls are adorned with the formal portraits of Catherine the Great (18th-century copy from the original by Dmitry Levitsky), her husband Peter III (18th-century copy from the original by Georg-Christoph Grooth) and Maria Fiodorovna, wife of Emperor Paul I (a work by Elizabeth Louise Vigée-Lebrun).

Unknown artist.
Portrait of Grand Duke
Peter Fiodorovich.
After 1743

Unknown Russian painter. ▶
Portrait of Empress Catherine II
as Legislator in the Temple of Themis.
Last quarter of the 18th century.

THE SECRETARY'S ROOM

The last room on the eastern side, the Secretary's Room, had a different name – the Choir Anteroom, as its door led to the court Church of SS Peter and Paul. Rastrelli adorned the Secretary's Room, like all the rooms of the main suite, with a lavish carved and gilt ornament on wooden panels, door surrounds and an overdoor; the walls were hung with silk. In the south western corner he placed a stove of "landscaped" tiles resting on lead gilt legs shaped like the heads of Bacchus with clusters of grapes symbolizing the autumn.

The most remarkable object in the Secretary's Room is its chandelier for 48 lights produced in 1851 for the Great Peterhof Palace at the Imperial Porcelain Factory in St Petersburg.

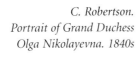

It was possible in the past to get through one of the doors of the Secretary's Room and the Blue Drawing-Room to the lavishly adorned and furnished rooms of the Eastern Wing. Today, however, this is impossible because of restoration work undertaken there. Another name of this section of the palace – Olga's Apartments – was supposed to remind about the year 1846 when these room s were prepared for the wedding of Nicholas I's daughter, Olga, with the Prince of Württemberg. Andrei Stakenschneider carried out a large amount of restoration work to create comfortable interiors for the newlyweds, who, though, did not live here long. Later the wing was often desolated and was used as a rule for receptions of official representatives of European monarchies and other notable guests.

*C. Robertson.
Portrait of Grand Duchess
Olga Nikolayevna. 1840s*

*Vase. The Imperial
Porcelain Factory,
St Petersburg.
1859*

*C. Robertson.
Portrait of Grand Duchess
Alexandra Nikolayevna. 1840s*

Today, a tour of the palace is continued through the rooms of the southern or garden enfilade. The next four rooms before the war were not included into the museum exhibition, although they retained, with some alterations, the decor made after sketches by Rastrelli. Having no concrete designation and often used for accommodating guests, these rooms have long since belonged to the Reserve Apartments. Two of these rooms have conventional parquet floors, while in two others the parquetry is adorned with an impressive pattern of large multi-radial stars. The lower wall panels in all the rooms were covered with gilt carved ornaments which echoed the design of the door leaves.

Rich silk hangings, the most remarkable decoration in these interiors, had a different pattern and colour scheme in each of the rooms. The wall hangings were repeatedly replaced, but the new silks produced by Russian weavers, continued to gladden the eye striking by their wealth and superb artistry. The Large Peterhof Palace excelled any other Russian palace in the luxury and variety of silk decorating its walls. It boasted about thirty fabrics of different design, colour and execution.

◀ *G. Dawe. Portrait of Grand Duke Nikolai Pavlovich*
(the future Emperor Nicholas I). 1820s

THE CROWN ROOM

The rooms adjoining the Oak Study on the east emerged after Rastrelli had added new blocks to Peter's Upper Mansion. The first, Crown Room, has retained of the original decoration only the parquet floor with an expressive Baroque "zigzag" ornament characteristic of many living rooms and halls of the palace. As a rule it was made of natural and water-seasoned oak, birch or maple. In 1770, this room was divided, after a project of Yury Velten, by a wooden partition forming a deep alcove and two rooms to the right and left of it. The architect

embellished the doors, the frame of the alcove and the overdoor apertures with a gilt carved ornament in the Classical style. As the room was connected by a passageway with a similar interior on the opposite, female half of the palace, the conclusion can be made that it was conceived as the Emperor's bedroom. However, its first occupant, Paul I, came to live here only a quarter of a century later. The architect Vincenzo Brenna designed on his instruction a special stand for the State Bedroom on which the imperial crown could be displayed during the Emperor's

Painted Chinese silk. 18th century

The recreation of the interior of the Crown Room was carried out after a drawing by Yury Velten. The ceiling was decorated with the painting *Venus and Adonis* by an unknown French artist of the eighteenth century.

The gilt state bedstead standing in the alcove is typical for eighteenth-century state bedrooms and was probably produced by an Italian craftsman. The two commodes with inlay decorations were made in Southern Germany in the middle of the eighteenth century.

*Armchair-toilet seat
with a pillow. Italy.
Early 18th century*

stay at Peterhof, and since that time the apartment became known as the Crown Room.

The room's silk, produced by Chinese weavers and artists in the late seventeenth or early eighteenth century, is interesting primarily by the subject matter of its painted decoration. It illustrates the entire technological process involved in the production of famous Chinese porcelain, the secrets of which then greatly intrigued Europeans.

*T*he western door leads from the Crown Room to Peter's part of the palace, to the room that has largely retained its decor of the first quarter of the eighteenth century. This is the famous Oak Study of Peter the Great, square in shape, with a low ceiling and four windows provided with oak shutters. Contemporaries noted the superb carved decorations of this interior. The Study is embellished with oak panels after a design by Jean-Baptiste Le Blond. The magnificent carved compositions on the walls were executed after drawings by the French sculptor Nicholas Pineau in 1718–20. At first twelve panels, overdoor decorations and door leaves were made. They were adorned with four figures personifying the seasons, various trophies of arms and musical instruments. Two of them carried profile representations of Peter the Great as a victor in a laurel wreath and of Catherine I in the guise of Minerva. The composition of the overdoor decoration was treated as a perfume-burner encircled by winged dragons. Pineau decorated the door leaves with depictions of herms.

*B. Coffre. Portrait
of Peter the Great.
1716*

In the middle of the eighteenth century the Study underwent alterations. A door leading to the newly built apartments was made in the eastern wall, a fireplace with a mirror was built instead of a stove and the nearby door leading to the room with a bed was blocked up. These changes led to the creation of new carved composition and the rearrangement of the earlier ones.

In 1941 eight panels, the door decorations were taken off and evacuated. Everything that had been left on the walls perished in fire. Now the recreation of the lost panels has been completed.

The furniture of the Study is similar to those pieces which stood here before the war. Of particular interest among Peter's personal belongings displayed in this room are books from his library and a table clock produced at the beginning of the eighteenth century by the Augsburg clock-maker Johannes Benner.

Clock. By J. Benner. Augsburg,
Germany. Early 18th century

he Oak Staircase has also survived from the Peter's times with minor alterations. Its name suggests the material used there not only for structural elements but for decoration as well. Jean-Baptiste Le Blond designed it as a rather compact three-flight structure in full accord with the original modest project of the palace. The staircase owes its elegance to elements of decor and especially to the oak balusters of the railing skilfully carved by Nicholas Pineau. In the middle of the eighteenth century Rastrelli increased the dimensions of the windows and the height of the staircase by piercing a large oval aperture in the ceiling. This aperture revealed a ceiling painting produced by Ivan Vishniakov in the same period. The painting featured the goddess of the dawn Aurora riding in a chariot.

The restored Oak Staircase is similar to the interior that had taken its final shape by the middle of the eighteenth century. On its western wall hangs a portrait of Peter the Great in a rich carved frame. It was probably painted from life by the Dutch court painter Benoît Coffre during Peter's visit to Copenhagen in 1716. It shows Peter as a military leader, in armour and ermine mantle, with a ribbon of the St Andrew Order across his shoulder. The Tsar's holds in his right hand the Marshal's baton and his left hand rests on the hilt of the sword. The portrait reminds us once again about the glorious history of the Fatherland and the great reformer of Russia, the founder of St Petersburg and Peterhof.

Decorative panel with representations
of Peter the Great after drawings
by N. Pineau. 1718–20

HE GREAT CASCADE

*The pool of the Sea Canal, the Great Cascade
and the Great Palace*

*The Upper Balustrade. Urns. After drawings
and models by A. Voronikhin. 1800.
Copies from ancient originals*

The majestic panoramic view of Peterhof opens from a distance, when one approaches it by sea. The most prominent landmark is the Great Palace which towers at the edge of a natural 16-metre terrace. At its slope the Great Cascade sparkles with the gold of its sculpture and the brilliance of its fountain jets. In front of the cascade, the powerful jet of the Samson Fountain bursts out in the centre of the pool, and further on water rushes towards the Gulf of Finland by the Sea Canal. Straight as an arrow, it lies on the north–south axis of the site.

The Great Cascade is the main structure of Peterhof's majestic fountain system. Remarkable for its dimensions, abundance of water, wealth of its sculptural decor, graphical variety of water jets, compositional unity and expressiveness of all parts, this magnificent example of Baroque art ranks among the best-known historical fountain structures of the world. This is a brilliant example of Baroque art. Its sculptures express in a figurative form the principal idea of the Peterhof ensemble – the celebration of Russia's glorious victories in the Northern War for the outlet to the Baltic shores.

The Great Cascade. Fountain:
Samson Rending Open the Jaws of
the Lion. Sculptor M. Kozlovsky. 1802

The centre of the Great Cascade is the Lower (Large) Grotto. Its outward wall, trimmed with tufa, is pierced by five high arches with gilt mascarons set up on their key-stones. The area in front of the Lower Grotto is flanked by two cascade stairways of seven steps adorned with gilt bas-reliefs, corbels, jets of water and gilt statues alternating with vases. In the centre of the area is the Basket Fountain, with its water running down the three waterfall steps to the pool. The wall of the Lower Grotto is completed by a granite cornice with a marble balustrade decorated with vases near the terrace of the Upper (Small) Grotto. The façade design of the latter shows an emphasis on the stylistic unity with the Great Palace: the decor is subordinate to its tripartite articulation, semicircular arches and niches, key-stones and the white-yellow colour of its painting. Another detail uniting these two structures is the balustrade marking the centre of the palace and also decorated with vases and echoing the design and material of the fence installed at the terrace of the Upper Grotto.

The present-day appearance of the cascade has taken shape in the course of a hundred years, but the concept of its composition was suggested by Peter the Great himself. The surviving sketches of the first Peterhof buildings drawn by the Tsar show that

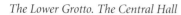

The Lower Grotto. The Central Hall

The ideas of Peter the Great about the creation of grottos with cascades fashionable in the 18th century were implemented by the architects Jean-Baptiste Le Blond, Johann Friedrich Braunstein and Niccolo Michetti. The building of the Great (Lower) Grotto was completed towards the middle of 1720. In 1721 Peter the Great ordered to make "a table with splashing" in the grotto. In 1723 the Emperor repeated his order about the creation of this trick fountain and gave instructions for creating water screens in the same place and for facing the grotto with tufa and shells

*The Lower Grotto. Pan and Olympius. The workshop of
J. Hamburger. St Petersburg. 1857. Copies from ancient originals*

*Pan, the Arcadian god of forests and groves, the son of Hermes,
danced and played his pipe, the sounds of which were identified
as the music of heavenly spheres*

Olympius, a shepherd, trained Pan to play the pipe

Peter was familiar with European structures of this kind. At the slope of the terrace he supposed to put up two grottoes and two cascade stairways with their water falling down to a rectangular pool connected by a canal with the sea. In 1715 the construction of the Sea Canal began, and in May 1716 the building of the Lower Grotto was started. The French architect Jean-Baptiste Le Blond, who then arrived in Peterhof, suggested, in order to make a stream of water more powerful, to place jets at the steps of the cascade, to change the shape of the pool making its semicircular and to widen the canal and fix its banks.

The earliest surviving depiction of Peterhof on an engraving by Andrei Rostovtsev allows us to form an idea of the original appearance of the Great Cascade. The principal details of its design have been retained throughout all later alterations: the Large

*The Lower Grotto. Venus Callypigos
("with fine hips"). The workshop of
J. Hamburger. St Petersburg. 1857.
Copy from an ancient original*

*The Lower Grotto. Bust: Winter.
Sculptor P. Baratta. 1717–18*

121

The eastern cascade stairway. Bas-relief: Perseus Liberating Andromeda

Perseus, the son of Zeus and Danaë, defeated the Gorgon Medusa and flying over the rock to which Andromeda was chained, saved her. This subject treats in an allegorical form the liberation of the Izhora lands – the fortresses of Yam, Nyenskans, Koporye and Narva (the four chains on Andromeda's arms and legs)

Grotto with an open ground over it, three waterfall stairways and a pool in front of them.

On Le Blond's death in 1719 the construction was supervised for a very short time by Johann Braunstein and during the next year Niccolo Michetti was put in charge of the project and continued the work. During the period of his supervision the grotto was decorated with stones and shells while the balustrade was embellished with vases. Somewhat later two mascarons, Bacchus and Neptune, appeared on the terrace over the Lower Grotto, and between them in the niches – marble busts featuring allegorical images of the four seasons. The Upper Grotto was also created there. Michetti reduced the number of the cascade steps to seven and decorated them with bas-reliefs.

The testing issue of water to the cascade took place on 13 July 1721 in the presence of Peter the Great. There was no sculptural decor yet, but the bas-reliefs were already being modelled. In the summer of 1723 three fountains and a table with a trick fountain were made in the Lower Grotto and the exit from the grotto was

Balustrade of the Upper Grotto. Vase.
After a drawing by A. Voronikhin. 1800

The Upper Grotto. Fountain mascaron.
18th century

The façade of the Upper Grotto.
Fountain mascaron: Neptune.
Modelled by C. B. Rastrelli after
a drawing by M. Zemtsov. 1724

The eastern cascade stairway. Bas-relief:
Pan with Satyrs and Cupids. A Bacchic Scene

The eastern cascade stairway

protected by a curtain of water jets. Seventeen jets of the Ring Fountain spurted out streams of waters in the centre of the area near the grotto.

In August 1723 the ceremony of the fountains' start-up was held – the Great Cascade began to function. But the work was continued. Soon the figures of *Perseus*, *Actaeon*, *Galatea* and *Mercury* and two mascarons appeared. In 1735, already after Peter's death, the Samson Fountain was set up in the centre of the pool; three years later a pair of tritons blowing sea-shells produced by Carlo Bartolomeo Rastrelli was installed at the marble stairway and the figures of two nymphs with dolphins were put on the sides of the pool. Thus the main amount of work on the decoration of the cascade was finished.

During the subsequent sixty years the cascade and the grotto were repeatedly repaired: the wooden pedestals were replaced with stone ones, the trimmings of the pools were renovated and the sculptures were given a new coat of gilding. Gradually many statues became decrepit and were a sorry sight, some of the bas-reliefs and decorative elements disappeared and the fountains in the grotto did not function.

Only at the end of the eighteenth century Paul I began to pay attention again to Peterhof. On 19 August 1799 he

The eastern cascade stairway.
Venus Callypigos. 1800.
Copy from an ancient original

The eastern cascade stairway. Perseus.
Modelled by F. Shchedrin. 1801

One of the exploits of Perseus, a hero of Argos legends, was his victory over the Gorgon Medusa who turned everything alive to stone. Perseus personifies Peter the Great who won a victory over Carl XII of Sweden

issued a decree that the lead pieces of sculpture be changed for bronze ones. The bronze statues were supposed to be close to the original ones and only in some cases it was permitted to create new sculptures. Fourteen statues – *Germanicus*, *Faun* (three), *Mercury* (two), *Ganymedes*, *Cerera*, *Venus* (two), *Discobolus*, *Amazon*, *Flora* and *Antinous* were produced from plaster casts of ancient originals preserved in the Imperial Academy of Arts; the group *Bacchus* and *Satyr* recreated the well-known work by Michelangelo. Several sculptures were cast from the original models by Russia's best sculptors of that period – Feodosy Shchedrin, Jean-Dominique Rachette, Fedot Shubin, Ivan Prokofyev and Ivan Martos. However, some of Carlo Bartolomeo Rastrelli's lead decorations – the bas-reliefs of the steps, the figures of frogs and mascarons – were retained. The four marble busts could also still be seen in the niches of the Upper Grotto.

Balustrade of the Upper Grotto. Vase.
After a model by A. Voronikhin and M. Kozlovsky. 1800
Copy from an ancient original

The sculptural group *Samson Rending Open the Jaws of the Lion* decorated the most powerful water jet of the Lower Park. A decision to construct this fountain was taken in 1734 when the twenty-fifth anniversary of the defeat of the Swedish troops at Poltava on 27 June 1709 was celebrated. This crucial event of the Northern War took place on the feast day of St Sampsonius which led to the allegorical depiction of the momentous battle in the form of a struggle of the Old Testament hero Samson with a lion. The sculptural group was to symbolize Russia's victory over Sweden which had a lion in its state emblem. In order to receive a jet of water as high as possible, the fountain master

Paul Sualem had a special wooden pipeline about four kilometres long laid from the Babigon Pond. In 1736 all the work was finished and the fountain began to spurt streams of water as high as twenty metres.

The sculptural group *Samson Rending Open the Jaws of the Lion*, cast in lead, was in need of a major repair ten years later and towards the end of the eighteenth century it became necessary to replace it. A notable Russian sculptor, Mikhail Kozlovsky, using the eighteenth-century composition, created a new model in classicizing forms, and the heroic subject became prominent at Peterhof again. Samson by Kozlovsky, cast in bronze, was set up on

127

The eastern cascade stairway. Flora. 1800.
Copy from an ancient original

Flora was the goddess of flowers, youth and pleasure

The eastern cascade stairway. Venus Callypigos. 1800.
Copy from an ancient original

Venus, the goddess of love and beauty born from the sea foam,
was a patroness of sea-faring

The western cascade stairway. Ganymede. 1800.
Copy from an ancient original

Ganymede, a beautiful son of the King of Troy, was abducted by Zeus who
carried the youth, disguised as an eagle, to heaven, bestowed immortality
upon him and made him the cupbearer

The western cascade stairway. Galatea.
After a model by J. D. Rachette. 1801

Galatea was a Nereid personifying a calm sea

The eastern cascade stairway. Pandora.
Modelled by F. Shubin. 1801

Zeus created Pandora as his revenge on Prometheus who stole fire
from heaven to give it to man. The god made Pandora beautiful
and insidious. Zeus gave her as a wedding present a vessel
containing all forms of human evils. Pandora opened it and
released them. Only Hope remained at the bottom of her vessel

The western cascade stairway. Acis. ▶
Model by I. Prokofyev. 1801

Acis, a Sicilian shepherd enamoured of Galatea, was
turned by the jealous Cyclops Polyphemus into a river

a pedestal made of granite slabs in 1802. At the hero's feet, as before, eight dolphins were frolicking and in niches near the pedestal were placed four half-figures of lions symbolizing the four points of the compass. In July 1806 the cascade was shown to the public in a renovated appearance.

The nineteenth century saw two major repairs of the Great Cascade. In the middle of the century, when it again became decrepit, the architect Andrei Stakenschneider offered a large-scale programme of its reconstruction. However, the cost turned out to be so large that his plan remained unrealized.

However, the restoration of the cascade became increasingly urgent every year and in 1859–60 it was begun under the supervision of Nikolai Benois. The main work was the erection of galleries for the examination of the fountain pipes and the making of special openings, lucarnes, for the ventilation of the grottos. The apertures pierced in the side walls of the cascade stairways were made for the same purpose. The architect changed the design of the Ring Fountain in front of the entrance to the Lower Grotto: it was now decorated with twenty-eight parabolic water-jets interlacing like in a basketwork which gave rise to the new title of the fountain, the Basket Fountain.

*The western
cascade stairway*

But Benois's plan was not entirely fulfilled. Attempts to recreate the removed tufa facing of the outer walls and interiors of the Lower Grotto, to restore the dismantled columns on the façade and to cover with marble the open grounds in front of the grottoes ended in failure. All this greatly distorted the original appearance of the famous structure. In 1861 efforts were made to recreate the lost decorative appearance of the grotto by placing there five galvanoplastic copies from ancient sculptures – *The Barberini Faun, Venus Callipygos, Cupid and Psyche, Bacchus* and *Pan and Olympus* – executed in the St Petersburg workshop of J. Gamburger.

The uncompleted restoration of the cascade soon made itself felt: at the beginning of the twentieth century it had a poor appearance again. However, restoration work on it was not carried until 1928. The pool and marble balustrade were then repaired, the partly lost decorative details of corbels and bas-reliefs were recreated.

The festive opening of the fountains at Peterhof after their restoration took place on 25 August 1946 and during the next season the powerful figure of *Samson Rending Open the Jaws of the Lion* appeared on its pedestal – it was reproduced from surviving photographs by the sculptor Vasily Simonov. The restoration of the pre-war fountains and sculptural decor was completed in 1950.

A new lease of life has been given to the Great Cascade in 1995, after seven-year restoration work. The restoration was necessary because of a decrepit state of the grottoes and underground communications supplying water to the cascade. The authors of the project decided also to recreate those details in the decor of the cascade which had been lost earlier,

Festivities at Peterhof

in the course of its long history. Their research was based on a scrupulous study of various documents: the drawings of the architects and fountain master craftsmen, eighteenth-century engravings and watercolours, archival sources and memoirs. The principal figurative material for the recreation of the lost details were axonometric plans drawn up by the well-known mathematician and cartographer Pierre de Saint-Hilaire in 1772–74 for

Ganymede and the Basket Fountain on the terrace ▶
near the Lower Grotto

The Basket Fountain. Designed by Nikolai Benois. 1860
Created on the site of the Ring Fountain designed by
Niccolo Michetti in 1723 on the orders of Peter the Great.
Fountain master Paul Joseph Soualem

The Great Cascade

Pool of the Sea Canal
Fountain group: Sirens. Sculptors F. Shchedrin,
A. Anisimov, I. Timofeyev. 1805

Sirens are half birds and half women
luring mariners by their sweet singing.
In the symbolism of the Great Cascade,
they eulogize, similarly to the naiads,
Samson's victory

The pool of the Sea Canal. The Volkhov River.
Modelled by I. Prokofyev. 1805

The pool of the Sea Canal. The Neva River.
Modelled by F. Shchedrin. 1805

The Neva in the guise of a young woman
and the Volkhov depicted as an old man are
allegorical representations of the two rivers
associated with a major event in Peter's
age – the construction of the Ladoga
Canal that linked them

View of the Western Voronikhin Colonnade
and the Sea Canal from the Great Cascade

Catherine the Great, as well as albums compiled in the late eighteenth century by A. Bazhenov and Piotr Neyelov. The ceremony of the start-up of the fountains of the renewed Great Cascade was held on 4 June 1995. On that day 138 jets of water spurted upwards and sparkled in the sun at Peterhof over one of the most perfect functioning fountain structures in the world.

The pool of the Sea Canal. Fountain: ▶
Samson Rending Open the Jaws of the Lion

The lead Samson sculpture was cast in 1735 after a model by Carlo Bartolomeo Rastrelli. The fountain master Paul Joseph Soualem, who laid a wooden four-kilometre pipe from the Babigon Pond for the future fountain set up at the feet of the Biblical hero eight dolphins spouting water and symbolizing the calm sea. Cast by Hans Conrad Ossner also after a model by Carlo Bartolomeo Rastrelli

$\mathcal{T}$HE CENTRAL PART OF THE LOWER PARK

The Bowl Fountains

The Terrace Fountains

The Great Cascade is flanked by small four-step cascades of white marble cut into the slope. There are five of them on each side and they are equally spaced along the entire width of the parterres. The alternating gilt mascarons of tritons and nymphs glisten in the upper walls of the cascades. They are fed with water from the fountains located on the ledge above. Each cascade corresponds to a fountain with a round marble pool and a small vertical jet. Water runs down the chutes laid along the terrace to the pool of the Great Cascade. The cascades were designed by Niccolo Michetti in 1722, but his plans were realized only at the end of the century, in 1799.

THE BOWL FOUNTAINS

At the foot of the terrace fountains, amidst the Great Parterres, are two much larger fountain structures known as the Bowl Fountains.

On 8 July 1721 an entry was made in Peter's *Field Journal*: "...His Majesty had a meal at Monplaisir and after the meal water was supplied to a fountain near the lower flower-beds which are near the Upper Mansion." This was the first setting into operation of the fountain which now can be seen in the centre of the western parterre. The piping and the pool for it were produced by two Italians, the Barratini brothers. The wooden bowls for

*The Voronikhin Colonnade.
Lion*

this fountain and its companion piece were made according to a design by Johann Braunstein and a model by Nicolas Pineau. The eastern fountain was put up by the Frenchman Paul Sualem and therefore it was called the French Fountain in contrast to its western counterpart, the Italian Fountain.

In 1854 stone-carvers at the Peterhof Lapidary Works, using a design by Andrei Stakenschneider, produced two bowls of Carrara marble to replace the old wooden ones. The Bowl Fountains play a significant part in the decoration of the Lower Park serving as a compositional balance to the huge water column of the Samson Fountain and articulating the space of the Great Parterres.

Собака гоняєтца заутками нашедь тогда уткии ей сказали тако напрасно ты печиса, тыдае сила имет еше насе гнатть то что непобеш силы не имаши.

The Favourite Fountain. Drawing made in M. Zemtsov's workshop. 1720s

THE FAVOURITE FOUNTAIN

The surviving Favourite Fountain is located behind the western Voronikhin Colonnade. There are always throngs of people near it. An amusing pug-dog and four ducks running away from him are moving around like in a circle dance. The dog's barking and the ducks' quacking never fail to attract Peterhof's guests. The meaning of the visual parable was explained by the following inscription: "The Favourite dog chased the ducks in the water, so the ducks said to her: 'All your efforts are in vain, you may have the strength to chase us, but not to catch us.'" Paul Sualem, who built this fountain in 1725 by order of Catherine I, placed a special water wheel at the bottom of the pool to set the dog and ducks in motion. Five years later the figures were replaced with painted copper ones.

Catherine's pug Favourite

THE VORONIKHIN COLONNADES

To the west and east of the Sea Canal are marble colonnades with pavilions crowned with gilt cupolas. The roof of each colonnade bears three gilt vases with fountains spurting water jets. Water pours down the cupolas into semicircular marble pools below. The Voronikhin Colonnades, as prominent architectural accents, give a sense of completeness to the entire ensemble of the parterre.

The first galleries with fountains were erected by Niccolo Michetti in wood and brick in 1722–23. By 1803 Andrei Voronikhin had put up brick colonnades on the site of the earlier galleries and decorated their stairways with four pairs of lions executed after a model by Ivan Prokofyev. In 1853–54 Andrei Stakenschneider faced the colonnades with marble and embellished the floors with Venetian mosaics.

In the remote north-western and north-eastern corners of the flower-beds are located semicircular benches of white marble executed in 1853–56 in the Pompeian style to a design by Andrei Stakenschneider. Behind them the architect placed shallow marble bowls with waterspouts. Each of the fountains is adorned in the centre with a female figure shining with gold: near the western bench he placed *Nymph*, a deity of source, a copy of the ancient Roman statue kept in the Hermitage, and embellished the eastern one with *Danaid*, a daughter of Danaüs, King of Argos, doomed to draw water ceaselessly, but in leaky jars which had to be forever refilled. The statue was cast in 1853 after a model by Ivan Vitali, who based it on the work of the German sculptor Christian Rauch.

The Danaid Fountain.
Mascaron

The Danaid Fountain

The Nymph Fountain ▶

THE WESTERN PART OF THE LOWER PARK

Eva

n the depth of the park, on the sides of the Sea Canal, there are two identically decorated fountains. The intersection of the avenues forms near them a sort of small squares, or *étoiles*, with eight rays diverging from them. Therefore these two large *étoiles* are very important features of the original layout of the Lower Park and it is not a mere chance that the oldest fountains of Peterhof are placed there – the Adam Fountain in the eastern part of the park and the Eve Fountain in the western one.

The *Field Journal* of Peter the Great contains a description of one of his recurrent visits to Peterhof in an entry for 30 June 1720: "He… was met by Her Majesty the Empress near a statue called *Adam* and she straightaway treated him to a glass of wine." *Adam* and its companion, *Eve*, were free copies from well-known works by Antonio Rizzi which decorate the staircase in the Doge's Palace in Venice to this day. Peter the Great ordered to commission them from the sculptor Giovanni Bonazza in 1717. The statues were set up in octahedral pools and encircled with sixteen jets of water. The Adam Fountain was completed by October 1722. The Eve Fountain, however, was finished and tested only in the autumn of 1726 and Peter could not see it working.

The Eve Fountain and a trellised arbour

In the course of more than 250 years the Adam and Eve Fountains have not undergone any major alterations and are the only fountains which retain their original architectural and sculptural decor from the age of Peter the Great.

The four trellised arbours which were put around the fountains as early as 1721 have a different history. In the middle of the eighteenth century the architect Francesco Bartolomeo Rastrelli replaced the decrepit structures with new ones and increased their number twice. Made in wood, the arbours were again in use for a short period, until the 1770s. The later attempts at restoration and recreation of Rastrelli's decorative structures ended in failure

The Adam Fountain

and it was only in 1802 that four new arbours were put up according to a design by the architect Franz Brouer. They were also built of wood, painted green and decorated with white columns and gilt details. The arbours had such an appearance until the Second World War. Destroyed during the occupation of Peterhof, two of the four arbours, near the Adam Fountain, were recreated in the 1970s and the other two, near the Eve Fountain, were reconstructed in 2000.

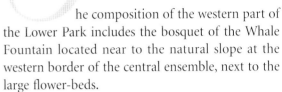
he composition of the western part of the Lower Park includes the bosquet of the Whale Fountain located near to the natural slope at the western border of the central ensemble, next to the large flower-beds.

Over the mirror-smooth surface of the large fancy-shaped pool spurts the eight-metre-high column of water around which are frolicking four gilt dolphins with jets of water gushing from their mouths too. This pool was designed by Niccolo Michetti after a concept of Peter the Great. Dug out and encircled with a dam in 1724–27 under the supervision of Vasily Tuvolkov, the pool stood without decor for sixteen years. In was only in 1739–40 that the Sand or Sterlet Pond, as it was then called, was decorated with painted sculpture, the focal element of which was the fairy-tale "Whale Fish with "sea bulls" on its sides.

At the end of the eighteenth century the dilapidating sculpture was removed and the fountain engineer Fiodor Strelnikov produced the fountain that functioned until 1885. The fountain has been recreated in 1963.

THE LION CASCADE

very palace had its corresponding cascade in the layout of the Lower Park. Therefore the idea to construct a cascade in the perspective of the avenue leading from the Hermitage Pavilion arose simultaneously with the erection of the New "Monplaisir" as the Hermitage was also called. The drawings of the fountain structure were made by the architect Niccolo Michetti as early as 1720, but he failed to realize his plan. Only at the end of the eighteenth century the idea of the "palace–cascade" compositional principle was fully realized to a design by Andrei Voronikhin.

The Lion Cascade.
Lion

The Lion Cascade. ▶
The nymph Aganippe

The architect placed the cascade between the Birch and Marly Avenues. Eight vases and the figures of *Heracles* and *Flora* were mounted on a low pedestal. A year later the latter two were replaced by two guarding lions. Streams of water from the vases flowed down into the upper pool and then by the steps to the lower pool. The cascade was named, according to its location, the Hermitage Cascade, but it had another name, after its sculptural decor, the Lion Cascade.

The Hermitage Cascade, as it was then known, existed until the middle of the nineteenth century. In 1854–55 a construction of the new cascade to a design by Andrei Stakenschneider began: a colonnade of fourteen eight-metre Ionic columns was placed on a granite basement repeating in plan the former cascade. The shafts of the columns were hewn from monolithic dark grey Serdobolye granite, while snow-white Carrara marble was used for their bases and capitals; twelve shallow bowls were produced of the same kind of marble at the Peterhof Lapidary Works. In the middle of the pool, on the hill of granite slabs stood the statue of the nymph Aganippe by the sculptor Fiodor Tolstoy. The nymph Aganippe was a mythological patron of the source near the Helicon mountain where the Muses used to gather. The nymph was pouring water from a jug and water jets spurted from the muzzles of colonnade of lions arranged on her sides. The Lion Cascade had similar appearance until 1941.

The Lion Cascade. Mascarons

THE HERMITAGE PAVILION

*I*n the depth of the avenue running slantwise from the Great Parterre to the north-west, on the seashore, there stands a slender two-storey edifice – the first "Hermitage" built in Russia. Over its entrance there is a balcony on carved corbels with a metal grille of elaborate pattern. The structure owes its unusual sense of lightness to the huge glazed doors, with light pouring freely through them. The building rests on a stylobate encircled with a deep moat. Only a light footbridge connects it with the outer world.

The Hermitage, which means "a secluded place" in French, was intended for a narrow circle of persons, the owner's personal friends. The idea of its construction came to Peter the Great during his travel around European countries where such pavilions were then fashionable. The construction of the Hermitage was commissioned to the architect Johann Braunstein and work be-

gan in 1721 to be completed, however, only after the Emperor's death, in the summer of 1725. Catherine I visited the pavilion on 25 July that same year. All in this building – the lift mechanisms, the two carved oak balconies and the dining-table for fourteen persons – was done according to her consort's project.

In the reign of Empress Anna Ioannovna the Hermitage was consigned to oblivion. And it was only Elizabeth Petrovna, the daughter of the founder of Peterhof, who remembered about her father's creation. During her reign Bartolomeo Francesco Rastrelli led work on the renovation of the lift mechanisms, new figures were carved for the pediments and in 1757–59 the walls were decorated with painting. Catherine the Great also often visited the Hermitage and enjoyed the time spent there. In 1766, in the narrow circle of the Empress's associates, the writer Denis Fonvizin read his satirical comedy *The Brigadier*.

The first storey of the pavilion is occupied by the Pantry and the Kitchen where dishes were warmed before being served. In the eighteenth century the upper floor could be reached only in a special chair-lift for two persons which was hoisted by a winch. This lift of a kind was in good working order until 1797, when, during a visit by Paul I and his family to the the Hermitage, the mechanism broke down and the members of the family could be evacuated only with the help of a ladder. The Emperor ordered to destroy the lifting mechanism and the present-day inner staircase was then built.

The Hall. The western wall.
Unknown Russian artist.
The Battle of Poltava.
First half of the 18th century

The Hall. The eastern wall.
G. Diziani. Antiochus and
Stratonice

The upper storey of the Hermitage is a vast Hall full of light and air. It was precisely for the sake of this vast interior that the whole building was erected. The Hall was intended for a narrow circle of the owner's most intimate friends who used to gather here. Fourteen people could sit in the centre of the room around the oval table with covers laid in front of each of them. The central section of the table with serving dishes was lifted from below through a special shaft, as described above. Any participant in the feast, however, could order a meal of his own. To this end, he was to state his wish in a note, put it on the plate and pull the string. Downstairs, in the Pantry, the bell rang and the servants lowered the plate through the shaft. A little later the plate with the ordered meal was sent back upstairs.

The main decoration of the Hall are 124 paintings by Western European artists of the 17th and the early 18th centuries. The pictures include battle scenes by Jacques Courtois, called Le Burguignon, marines by Michiel Maddersteeg and Ludolf Backhuyzen, landscapes by Matthias Withoos and Gerrit Berckheyde, everyday scenes by Jan Miense Molenaer and Egert van Heemskerck, the bright, colourful pictures by Gaspard Peter Verbruggen and Pieter van Bloumen, the representations of the Apostles by the Dutch artist Georg Gsell, who was invited by Peter the Great to serve in Russia and spent 23 years in this country. Noteworthy among Italian paintings are *Antiochus and Stratonice* by Gasparo Dizziani, one of the best canvases in the Hermitage collection, works by Giulio Carpioni and one of the most significant works in the collection is *The Death of Cato* by Luca Giordano. A historical subject is treated by another Dutch painter of the seventeenth century, Nicolaes Rosendael, whose painting decorates the shield of the fireplace. The only work in the Hermitage collection produced in Russia is *The Battle of Poltava*, painted by an anonymous Russian master in the eighteenth century.

A small but representative and diverse collection of the Hermitage allows the visitor not only to see the world through the eyes of the artists of the seventeenth and eighteenth centuries, but also to have some idea about the collecting of the fine arts in Russia during that period.

The Hall

The Hall. The northern wall.
G. Berckheyde. Town Street

The Hall. The northern wall.
G. de Lairesse. Antony and Cleopatra

The Hall. The eastern wall.
J. M. Molenaer. Village Wedding

The Hall. The southern wall.
M. Withoos. View of a Park

The Hall.
The northern
wall.
G. Gsell.
The Apostle
Paul

THE MARLY
ENSEMBLE

he Marly Ensemble owed its name to the residence of the French kings, Marly-le Roi near Paris. The Marly Palace is the main structure in the Lower Park. Although not large, it plays an important role in the overall composition of the park. Three main avenues diverge from the palace like rays cutting the park from west to east: the central Marly Avenue, the northern Maliebaan Walk and the southern Birch Alley. The radiating avenues lead not only to the structures located there – the Hermitage Palace or Pavilion, the Eve Fountain and the Lion Cascade, but, crossing the Sea Canal, compositionally link this part of the park with the Adam Fountain and the ensemble of Monplaisir on the one side and the Chessboard Hill Cascade on the other. At the same time the Marly Palace is the focal centre of a relatively autonomous architectural complex including a pond, two gardens (the Venus and Parterre Gardens), a cascade and fountains on the parterre in front of the edifice.

The silhouette of Marly is visible from a large distance. Its relatively modest, but exquisite façade, with a high roof and the tracery of balcony grilles, is reflected, like a fairy-tale vision, in the calm waters.

The Garden of Venus. Venus.
Copy from an ancient original

The work began in 1720 was completed by 1722. Construction work started with the building of two ponds, the rectangular Marly Pond and a semicircular one. The excavated soil was employed to raise a huge rampart along the gulf, which could serve both as a dam and as a barrier against northern winds. The semicircular pond with three radial brick partitions was divided into four sectors, hence its later name, the Sectorial Ponds. The artificial ponds, in addition to aesthetic purposes, had purely economical functions – to rear crucians and other kinds of carp and pike-perch. The area between the northern bank of the Marly Pond and the earth rampart was used to lay out the Venus Garden where fruit trees, berry shrubs and flowers were planted. In the niches of the breast-walls cherry-trees were grown and in the centre of the garden stood a statue of the goddess of love. Another garden was laid out on the opposite bank of the pond. Here in 1721, on the slope of a hill, the construction of a cascade was started and two parterre fountains were installed. Later, four cloche fountains were added to them.

Vases at the Marly Avenue. ▶
After a model by A.Voronikhin. 1805

THE GOLDEN HILL CASCADE

The steps of white marble descending from the height of 14 metres, the gilt sheets of risers, the sculpture and, finally, the stone staircases with balustrades, all this makes the cascade exceedingly effective. A statue of *Neptune* holding a trident in his hands decorates its upper wall and it is flanked by *Triton* blowing a sea shell and *Bacchus*, the god of wine. Under each piece of sculpture gilt masks of sea monsters can be seen with streams of water shooting out of their open jaws and flowing down the steps.

Drawing on detailed instructions of Peter the Great, Niccolo Michetti worked out a project which was completed by the Russian architect Mikhail Zemtsov in 1732. In addition to the masks, which had been set up on the upper wall by that time, the architect added sculptures on the attic and in the pool; he also hung gilt sheets under the steps which created a vivid play of light through the mirror of falling water. From that time onwards the cascade came to be called the Golden Cascade.

In 1870 the cascade was repaired under the supervision of Nikolai Benois. The lead sculptures were then replaced for marble ones bought in Italy.

The Golden Hill Cascade.
Sculptural decor
of the attic

The Golden Hill Cascade

THE MÉNAGÈRES
FOUNTAINS

lthough they the parterre fountains compositionally matching the Golden Hill were created by Peter the Great himself, they came to be called the Ménagères Fountains only in the middle of the nineteenth century. Ménagère means 'economical' in French. The huge 15-metre-high columns of water produce the impression of abundant streams, although they are hollow inside. The nozzle of each fountain is thirty centimetres in diameter, but there is a blocking cone inside which leaves a circular gap several centimeters wide near the walls of the pipe for the water to pass through. Water, flowing through the cone, bursts out under great pressure. The nozzles were cast and fixed to the fountain pipes according to Peter's own drawings. Their design has reached us with no major alterations.

◀ *The Ménagères Fountains*

The Cloche Triton Fountain

THE CLOCHE FOUNTAINS

n 1724 it was planned to build four fountains based on subjects borrowed from Aesop's fables near the Ménagères Fountains. However, several years later the original plan was altered in favour of four figures of tritons. The tritons had been cast in bronze in England in 1721 after a drawing by Johann Braunstein and were intended for the Great Cascade. The heads of the tritons supported lead-lined wooden bowls provided with four small pipes through which water was to burst out. At the end of the eighteenth century the bowls were replaced with flat disks each of which had a pipe with a nozzle. A stream of water gushing through the pipe took the form of a bell. Hence the name of the Cloche Fountains – *cloche* means 'bell' in French. In 1912 the pools of Pudost marble were replaced for granite ones but exactly repeating the outlines of the former pools.

*The Golden Hill. Faun. 19th-century
copy from an ancient original*

173

THE MARLY PALACE

The construction of the Marly Palace began in 1720, when the work of excavating soil from the large pond was nearing completion. The project of the "Minor Seaside Palace", as it was mentioned in initial documents, was designed by Johann Braunstein. According to the initial concept, the building was to have one storey. However, in 1721, when the building was already provided with a roof, Peter the Great ordered that another storey be added. By 1723 the upper storey was built and within the next year decorative work in the interiors was mainly completed.

The palace was intended for "celebrated persons". But already from the middle of the eighteenth century it was turned into a repository of objects associated with Peter the Great. It was used to keep his wardrobe, presents made to him, everyday objects, paintings, furniture, etc.

For nearly two centuries Marly did not undergo any major alterations. But in the nineteenth century dangerous cracks appeared on its walls. On the suggestion of the architect Alexander Semionov, after careful measurements and removal of the interior decoration, the building was dismantled down to its foundations and then reassembled, after the foundations had been reinforced, from similar materials. Then the decor was restored in keeping with its former design.

◄ *The Giustiniani Athena. Sculptor F. Francci. 1846.*
Copy from an ancient original

175

The ground plan of the Marly Palace is unusual. It has no traditional formal hall common for such kind of palaces. A long Corridor with doors on either side leading to dwelling premises and auxiliary rooms extends from the Vestibule. Both storeys are similar in design, but the ground floor, which is much higher, has always been regarded as a state one.

Today, visitors enter the palace from the Sectorial Ponds and begin their acquaintance with the museum from auxiliary rooms located on the left side of the Corridor.

The Kitchen of the Marly Palace was built in the "Dutch manner": the huge hooded stove in the corner, the marble floor and the walls faced with tiles from top to bottom. The tiles in this room – pictorial compositions in cobalt blue featuring various Dutch landscapes and scenes enclosed in lilac-coloured frames with representations of carnations or lilies at their corners – are vivid. On the shelves, tables and the stove are typical kitchen utensils of the first half of the eighteenth century – English tinware, German vessels, copper cauldrons and pots made at the Urals factories, Dutch and German pottery.

The Kitchen adjoins a small room without any decor, where, in former times, tableware and linen were kept. The single-tone decor of the walls is enlivened by multicoloured vessels. Hanging on the walls are mid-seventeenth-century porcelain Chinese dishes decorated in cobalt blue, and next to them, faience plates produced a century later at Delft and Frankfurt-am-Main in imitation of Oriental wares. Set on the shelves of the dresser are Japanese and Chinese plates with bright painted decoration, bottles, goblets and wine-glasses of Russian and Western European work. Of particular interest are flasks of dark brown glass intended for mineral water which, as legend has it, were brought by Peter the Great from Spa in Flanders, where he underwent treatment. The dark bottles inscribed Danzig and London on their seals also belonged to the Emperor. They were used for wine, and the seals indicated the country where the wine was produced. The furniture in the Pantry – the sideboard, the wash-stand, the dresser and the carved sgabello chairs – is characteristic of Peter's palaces and was marked by heavy forms and simplicity of design.

The Dining-Room

177

The Entrance Hall

The Entrance Hall is the largest room in the palace, with a stone floor and a fireplace in the north-western corner. In past times, the main entrance to the palace was from the Marly Pond and led to this room, the vestibule, which was intended by Peter the Great as a formal Entrance Hall. According to the initial project, it was supposed to embellish the ceiling with an ornament and to pane the entrance door with "Yamburg glass for viewing perspectives". But the concept changed and the ceiling was left smooth. Only the coving was decorated with fine moulding. Small two-colour reliefs depicting seaside towns and harbours were placed between the companion brackets. In the course of the postwar restoration, however, the reliefs were not reconstructed and their place is merely indicated by a colour.

In the nineteenth century the vestibule became known as the Entrance Hall or Anteroom. Its furnishing was very simple – a number of chairs and a large table. Today, the Entrance Hall is decorated with marquetry furniture which was produced by Dutch masters in the first half of the eighteenth century.

The decor of the room is supplemented by works of painting which invariably were an important feature of Peter the Great's palatial interiors. He purchased pictures for his future palaces himself at sales in Amsterdam or ordered them through his agents in Holland and Italy. Jacob Stählin, Academician of the Russian Academy of Sciences, left a record of the Marly collection of painting in 1738–39. The palace housed then 45 paintings by Dutch, Flemish, Italian and German artists. Some of the canvases were taken away from Marly in the eighteenth century, others were destroyed by a fire in 1901 and five were stolen by the Nazi soldiers during the Second World War. The present-day collection includes about thirty paintings from the initial display. Six of them are in the Entrance Hall: two companion paintings *Herdsmen and a Herd* by Philipp Peter Roos, a German artist who lived in Italy; two still lifes with fruit by an unknown Dutch artist and twin portraits of an old man and an old woman by the Italian painter Pietro Belotto.

The Entrance Hall. A. Celesti. Christ and the Adulteress

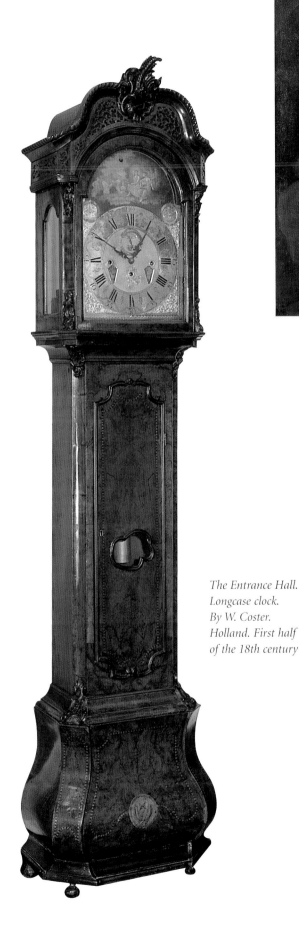

The Entrance Hall. Longcase clock. By W. Coster. Holland. First half of the 18th century

Although the two other paintings on the western wall have been transferred to Marly quite recently, after the Second World War, they were among Peter's purchases for the Summer Palace in St Petersburg. Both paintings are devoted to Biblical subjects. One is *Christ Preaching in the Temple* by the Italian artist Tiziano Vecellio, called Il Tizianello, and the other *Christ and the Adulteress* by another Italian, Andrea Celesti.

Between the Entrance Hall and the Bedroom there is a small room with a single window, the Duty Room, which was intended for an officer on duty. In Peter's palaces, such rooms were commonly located near the Bedroom. A small moulded cornice and flat reliefs depicting armorial trophies make up the entire decor of this interior. However, as in other rooms, painting plays a significant part in this interior too. Remarkable among paintings hung in the Duty Room are works by Dutch artists – *Morning* by Rinse Verzyll and an animal scene by Adriaen van Oolen. Both pictures have come from Peter's collection.

The walls in the Bedroom, as in Peter the Great's other palaces, are lined with a fabric. In this case a cotton print with a characteristic "grass" motif has been used. In the course of the two centuries it was renovated several times, but the original design was invariably exactly repeated. The same fabric was used for lining a large bed designed "in the French manner", with a canopy over it and covered by Peter's quilted blanket finely embroidered with a representation of Venus's chariot. Of particular note in this room is the banquette which stands near the bed and is, at first glance, unworthy of attention. It is one of the six similar seats which were used in the palace from its very beginning. Its fragments found in the basement of the palace after the war were

assembled and the restored banquette was used as a model for the reconstruction of the entire set.

A small room following the Bedroom, with a window facing the Sectorial Ponds, is the Plane Study, named so because it is faced with beautiful iridescent panels of planewood.

Campredon, the French ambassador to the Russian court, in his report to the king about his visit to Peterhof, made a special emphasis on the decor of the Plane Study, although he erroneously identified the wood which decorated the interior as "the cedar of Persia". In actual fact, however, the planewood was sent to St Petersburg by Artemy Volynsky, the governor of Astrakhan, and was kept in the Admiralty warehouse for a long time. Only several years later it was used by Peter the Great for the decoration of a room in the Marly Palace. On the southern, eastern and northern walls are three portraits of Peter the Great's children – the companion likenesses of Anna and Elisabeth as well as a portrait of Alexis with the attributes of war and of Piotr with the attributes of peace.

Owing to its small size, this room could accommodate only a bureau and a chair.

One of the doors of the Bedchamber opens to the Lower Corridor, at the end of which, by the exit to the Sectorial Ponds, there is a staircase leading to the first floor. Its two flights with winding steps at the turn were faced with oak and the handrails were made of wrought-iron with gilt details and of burnished steel. Amazingly elaborate pattern of the handrail featuring Peter's monogram,

The Dressing-Room. The caftan of Peter the Great embroidered with the star of the Order of St Andrew the First-Called

birds and tropheys suggests that it was created by Nicolas Pineau, who produced sketches for the grilles of the palace's balconies.

At the first floor, opposite the staircase there is a tiny Wardrobe Room, where in past times some part of Peter's extensive wardrobe, which comprised 300 items, was housed. The bulk of Peter the Great's clothes was transferred, in the reign of Nicholas I, to the Imperial Hermitage in St Petersburg, but even today the Peterhof collections own some interesting garments which belonged to the Emperor.

The handrail of the Staircase. After a sketch by N. Pineau. By S. and P. Yakovlev. 1722. Russia. The Crown of the Russian Empire

The Upper Corridor leading to the rooms of the first floor is decorated, like the ground floor, with paintings by Dutch and Flemish artists of the seventeenth and early eighteenth centuries.

The door in the northern wall of the Corridor leads to the Dressing-Room, the southern one to the Drawing-Room and that at the end of the Corridor to the Dining-Room. All these interiors have smoothly plastered walls decorated with tonal painting, unsophisticated cornices and a parquet floor with a simple pattern; there are also two small corner fireplaces. The Dressing-Room, which is sometimes called the Wardrobe Room, because once it had been employed for keeping Peter the Great's private belongings, is much larger than the other room intended for this purpose. The cupboard of Dutch work and a massive Italian chest for keeping clothes account for the name of this room.

The choice of furniture which had formerly decorated the Drawing-Room and the small Corner Room adjacent to it, was rather casual and consisted of separate items made in the eighteenth century. At present the Dressing-Room attracts viewers' attention by its rich cabinet, trimmed with mother-of-pearls and tortoise-shell over a gold leaf, a work by eighteenth-century Dutch cabinet-makers.

The largest room of the first floor was the Dining-Room located above the Entrance Hall. The glazed door of the room leading to the balcony, which affords a splendid view of the Marly Palace and the three diverging avenues, is located on the axis of the palace and so this vista with a perspective view behind the windows can be seen already from one's first steps along the Corridor. In the centre of the room there always stood a huge table occupying most of its space, the walls were decorated with "perspective architectural paintings with large gardens in the foreground", painted by the Italian artists and purchased on the order of Peter the Great. The side doors led to the Oak Study and the Library.

Unlike its counterpart in the Great Palace, the Oak Study in the Marly Palace created to the designs of Johann Braunstein, was covered with smooth oak panels and only after they were fitted the strikingly expressive mascarons in carved ornamental frames were installed. The carved decor was most probably designed by Nicolas Pineau. On the pilaster strips between the panels miniature twin carved tropheys

The Dressing-Room. A. Silo. Ships Riding at Anchor

The Oak Study

were placed. The furnishings of the Study were unassuming and practical – a Dutch bureau adorned with an ivory inlay, books and a clock on its top, an armchair next to it and a table near the window. According to tradition, the table decorated with carved wood and a slate inset was made with the participation of Peter the Great himself.

Peter the Great's contemporaries, who visited his palaces, paid attention to the fact that in all of them the Emperor had small subsidiary libraries, right in his studies or nearby. In the Marly Palace a separate room was allotted for books. Peter's libraries usually included books on navigation, mathematics, park gardening, geographical atlases, etc. Today they are preserved in the English-made bookcase of the early eighteenth century. The globe standing in the Library was also produced in England at the same time. Visitors can see on the wall the painting Sea Port with the City Gate of Rotterdam by the Dutch artist Abraham Storck.

The Drawing-Room. A. Grevenbroeck.
Sea Harbour

The Library.
A. Storck.
Sea Port
with the City
Gate of
Rotterdam

THE WESTERN PART OF THE LOWER PARK

The Great Orangery

THE ORANGERY FOUNTAIN

To the east of the Great Parterres, by the foot of the terrace lies a small oval garden with flower-beds, fruit trees and a fountain in the centre. On the southern side it adjoins the richly decorated façade of the Great Orangery built to a design by Johann Braunstein in 1722–25. Although the structures looked like palaces, the building was used for distinctly utilitarian purposes: for growing grapevines, melons, citrus plants, etc.

In the centre of the Orangery Garden, in a round pool, stands a gilt sculptural group featuring a mighty triton rending the jaws of a sea monster, with a powerful jet of water gushing upwards from the monster's mouth. Smaller streams are shooting from the peer-ing out heads of the turtles which are placed at the four corners of the islet symbolizing the points of the compass.

In 1726 the sculpture, produced to a design by Timofei Usov and after a model of Carlo Bartolomeo Rastrelli, was cast in lead and in 1876 the worn-out lead group was replaced with a different composition, *Satyr and a Crocodile*. In the post-war years, however, the original sculptural decor was recreated after a drawing found in an eighteenth-century art book. The artistic concept of Rastrelli's composition had much in common with the sculpture of the Samson Fountain. The Orangery Fountain was also designed as a reminder of the victory in the war against the Swedes in the Northern War.

The Orangery Fountain ▶

*Apollo.
Copy from an ancient original*

THE ROMAN FOUNTAINS

These are hardly not the most beautiful fountains at Peterhof. They have the form of two-step composition: on a massive marble cubic pedestal rests a huge disc and it supports a smaller pedestal, also with a disc, from the centre of which spurt five jets of water forming a sort of many-stepped pyramid. The Roman Fountains are a beautiful decoration of the square and resemble pylons flanking an exit to the Monplaisir Avenue.

They were created in 1738–39 to designs by Johann Blank and Ivan Davydov. The fountain master Paul Sualem was responsible for the piping. In 1756 Francesco Bartolomeo Rastrelli, retaining the basic idea of the fountains, developed a new architectural project replacing, in particular, the former bowls for discs. At first this project was realized in wood and only in 1800 a stone version came into being. Various kinds of coloured marbles and sculptural works in the form of garlands shining with gold, wreathes and masks cast after models by Ivan Martos were used to adorn the fountains in 1817. These fountains were thought to look like those which decorate the square in front of the Cathedral of St Peter in Rome, hence their name.

THE CHESSBOARD
HILL CASCADE

The Chessboard Hill Cascade, another remarkable feature of the Lower Park, stands near the Roman Fountains and water falling down from the cascade flows in their direction. At its top and bottom are entrances to the grottoes. Three dragons are put on guard near the Upper Grotto. Powerful streams of water are shooting from their open jaws to flow down the four huge inclined steps. The slopes of the cascade are laid with tufa and set up along the wooden stairways are ten marble statues; effigies of ancient deities produced by Italian sculptors.

The construction of the cascade began soon after the Palace of Monplaisir had been founded. Peter the Great ordered "to produce a small grotto" and Niccolo Michetti made its design based on the Tsar's detailed description. As early as 1724 marble sculptures intended for the slopes of the hill arrived from Italy. After the death of Peter the Great work on the construction of the Small Grotto, or the Ruin Cascade as it was sometimes called, proceeded slowly and was often halted. At last, by the year 1739, the cascade had been completed to a design by Mikhail Zemtsov and was called the Dragon Hill Cascade. In the middle of the eighteenth century its steps were painted to imitate a chessboard pattern and it became known as the Chessboard Hill Cascade.

The Chessboard Hill Cascade.
Pluto. Italian sculptor
of the early 18th century

The Chessboard Hill Cascade.
Dragon

In the first half of the nineteenth century the cascade was repeatedly repaired. In 1855 Nikolai Benois was entrusted to work out a design for "the construction of the Dragon Hill Cascade anew". The court architect offered several versions of its renovation which were directed mainly at reinforcing its walls, the foundations of the steps, etc.

It was, however, only in 1875 that the wooden dragons were replaced according to Benois's drawing with metal ones, a large eagle was mounted over the Upper Grotto and a galvanoplastic copy of the group *Nymph and Satyr* by the sculptor Piotr Stavasser was erected in the pool by the Lower Grotto. The structure had such appearance until 1941. Reconstructing the cascade, restorers recreated the appearance it had in the middle of the eighteenth century: relying on late-eighteenth-century drawings they only installed dragons by the entrance to the Upper Grotto. The surviving marble sculptural pieces were set up on their former places.

THE PYRAMID FOUNTAIN

In the eastern part of the Lower Park, on a side avenue, a fountain can be seen, that is especially striking for its great number of water jets and unusual pattern. It resembles a triumphal structure from a distance. In 1717 Peter the Great, on a visit to France, took an interest in the fountain shaped as three-edged obelisk. In 1721, after a complete victory over the Swedes in the Northern War, he recalled this water monument and entrusted Niccolo Michetti to repeat the Versailles project. Three years later the Pyramid Fountain, as the fountain with cascades on its four sides was called, was put into operation. The principle of its functioning is very simple and has been left intact throughout its long existence. The pyramidal effect is achieved by means of a gradual lessening of a diameter of 505 copper pipes towards the centre – the pressure of water rises and, correspondingly, jets spurt higher. In 1799–1800 a marble balustrade was mounted around the water obelisk and decorative vases were set up.

◄ *The Pyramid Fountain*

The Fir Trick
Fountain

Trick Fountain: The Road

THE TRICK FOUNTAINS

F rom the square in front of the Chessboard Hill Cascade to the Monplaisir Garden leads the straight and wide Monplaisir Avenue. Recreated here in 2000 was the large-scale trick fountain originally conceived by Peter the Great and lost in the middle of the eighteenth century. The amusement called *The Road*, is a large *berceau* of water jets that suddenly begin to burst out on either side of the road covering it with hundreds of watery arches.

In the past water amusements could be met practically in every regular park. But Peterhof is unrivalled in the number of such fountains today. For example, the Oak Fountain has five tulips and two benches near them. A visitor, walking in the park at the height of summer, would like to see the tulip flowering so late, bend down to admire it, to be only surprised by a shower of water. In bewilderment, the guest would step back to find protection under the tree but the "oak" made of hollow pipes, would instant-

ly come alive with water shooting from its leaves and branches. Taken aback, he would head to the benches but streams of water would hit him there too. Similar scenes can be seen today. In 1735 the Oak Fountain was installed in a pool of the Upper Gardens and in 1802 it was transferred to the Lower Park. Next to it there are three artificial fir-trees, made in 1784, whose branches spout silvery streams of water.

Almost opposite the Oak Fountain, on the other side of the Monplaisir Avenue, stands a round bench. The pillar rising over it is crowned with a canopy reminiscent of an umbrella. A pipe with 164 openings is disguised along the edge of the canopy. Once you sit at the bench, the fountain begins to operate and you cannot escape the wall of downward jets without getting wet. The Umbrella Fountain, or the Chinese Fountain as it was also called, was put up in the park in 1796.

The Umbrella
Trick Fountain

frequent attribute of many regular gardens in the early eighteenth century was a place where exotic animals and birds were kept. According to Peter's concept, something of this kind was included into the complex of the Monplaisir structures under the French name of Ménagerie. A vast pond was dug out for waterfowl in 1718–19. Ducks, geese and swans could be seen in it as well as huge sturgeons brought to the imperial gardens from the Volga. Two years later a fountain was installed in it. Next to the Ménagerie Pavilions, in the centre of a large pool there is an original and technically complicated fountain, *The Sun*. On a round pedestal stands a fluted pillar, which is surrounded by sixteen dolphins spouting out streams of water from their jaws. The slowly rotating pillar has three parallel gilt discs at its top shooting jets of water.

The pool in which the Sun Fountain is installed was dug out during the period when Peter's Ménagerie was placed there. In 1721–24, by order of Peter the Great, Niccolo Michetti built a fountain in the centre of the pool with twelve arc-shaped jets around the central column of water rising from the surface of the pool. A half a century later, Yury Velten redesigned the reservoir into a bathing-pool and encircled it with high walls lining them with canvas on either side and decorating with painting on the side facing the park. The fountain was also changed: a round pedestal was installed in the centre of the pool and sixteen dolphins were mounted on it. In front of them, in the basement chamber of the pedestal, a wheel put into motion by water was placed. This turbine rotated, in turn, the pillar at the top of which were placed three parallel discs with 187 openings. The jets of water shooting from them were reminiscent of the rays of sunlight and therefore the fountain became known as the Sun Fountain. In 1925 the walls of the bathing-pool were dismantled.

Cupid Riding a Dolphin.
Sculptor C. Angelini. 1848

The Sun Fountain.
Dolphins

Psyche. 1870. Copy from
the original by A. Canova ▶

n the eastern part of the Lower Park, in front of the south façade of the Palace of Monplaisir, there stretches the Monplaisir Garden with flower parterres and fountains. One of the Emperor's drawings dating from the start of the Peterhof construction, contains the plan of a garden near the "chambers" standing on the seashore. The two avenues crossing at the right angle divide the rectangular space into four parterres. The sheet bears the inscription in Peter's hand instructing how to plant flower-beds. As early as 1718 limes, chestnut-trees and maples were planted and trellises were made. The lawns, however, still lacked flower-beds – they appeared in the Monplaisir Garden only in the middle of the eighteenth century. But tulips, an indispensable feature of Dutch gardens, were planted there every year. The tract of land was also embellished with small heat-loving trees in beautiful vases painted in cobalt blue.

In August 1721 Peter thee Great gave precise instructions about the arrangement of the fountain system. In 1721 Michetti worked out a design of the garden using the Tsar's detailed descriptions and sketches. The focus of the composition is the Sheaf Fountain. A powerful stream of water gushes from a pedestal which bears resemblance to a bundle of ears. Its effect is enhanced by 24 parabolic jets encircling the centrepiece in two tiers. In the past, the Sheaf Fountain was flanked with four cloche fountains decorated with copies from ancient sculptures *Apollino* and *Ganymede* as well as with *Faun* by Giovanni Rosso and *Bacchus* by Jacopo Sansovino. The statues were placed on pedestals shaped as overturned bowls from which water flowed down. In 1817 the earlier lead statues were replaced with new ones, cast in bronze after models by Ivan Martos. Only one new statue, that of *Psyche*, was put instead of *Ganymede*, all the rest repeated the former subjects.

Two modest white benches with gilt masks of tritons on their backs invariably attract many visitors to the Monplaisir Garden. These are the famous Peter's trick fountains produced from the Tsar's drawings and tested as early as 1723. When ladies and cavaliers intoxicated by merry-making would go out of doors to refresh themselves and head to the benches, they found themselves under a shower of thin streams of water.

◀ *The Cloche Psyche Fountain*

The Bench
Trick Fountain

The Cloche Faun
Fountain

The Monplaisir
Garden

J. Meyer. Terrace at the Palace ▶ ▶
of Monplaisir. 1843

The ensemble of the eastern section of the Lower Park occupies a large territory and is richly decorated with sculptures and fountains. Its main architectural landmark and the focal point of its layout, however, is the Palace of Monplaisir with three avenues radiating from it. The main one, the Monplaisir Avenue, runs towards the Chessboard Hill Cascade and two others lead to the Adam and Pyramid Fountains. Unlike the Great Palace, the Palace of Monplaisir is located at the edge of the Gulf of Finland.

A magnificent picture unfolds before visitors arriving to Peterhof by sea: a high terrace reinforced with huge granite boulders and encircled by an elegant white balustrade echoing the outline of a single-storey brick building with a tall roof. This is Peter the Great's palace called Monplaisir. Attached to its central block are two recessed galleries with structures known as lusthhaus pavilions. The walls of the galleries are pierced with narrow glassed doors alternating with deep semicircular niches emphasizing the massive bulk of the walls which protect the area from the northern wind.

The palace has an absolutely different look from the southern side: the galleries are aligned with the central volume of the structure and form a kind of graceful arcade with streams of light pouring in through their glazed apertures. In front of the palace stretches a cosy garden with flower-beds and fountains. On the eastern side it is limited by the Guest Gallery, the Bath House and the Assembly Hall with auxiliary premises. On the western side are a similar gallery and a spacious palace known as the Catherine Block.

The complex took its shape mainly towards the mid-eighteenth century. It is called Monplaisir ("my pleasure" in French) and derives its name from Peter the Great's small amusement palace, although previously the building had been called the Dutch House for the resemblance of its layout and its façade and interior decoration to small "burgher" dwellings in Holland.

The Hall

213

Monplaisir is as old as Peterhof itself. The history of the whole palace and park ensemble began with the construction of Monplaisir. The palace was Peter the Great's favourite creation, and it was he who gave it this name. The Emperor himself chose the site for the construction and sketched the layout of the building. It is hardly possible to find any other place where his personal habits and tastes could be so strongly felt.

As is the case with a number of other monuments dating from the first quarter of the eighteenth century, no reliable data on the designer of the palace of Monplaisir have reached us. Many researchers are inclined to believe that it was designed by Andreas Schlüter, an architect who worked in Russia for some time before his death in 1714. In any case, his assistant and pupil Johann Braunstein was responsible for the building work and interior decoration there.

The construction of the palace began in May 1714 and by August 1723, when the first gala festivities were held in Peterhof, Monplaisir had been completed.

During Peter the Great's last years Monplaisir was used for small receptions. In the mid-eighteenth century, although tea-drinking parties and intimate dinners were held in the palace, it was above all regarded as "one of the most revered relics of national history".

Visitors' tour of the museum begins from The Lusthaus, a small pavilion known by the German name *Lusthaus* (the amusement house). The Eastern Lusthaus, square in plan, with a brick floor and four huge doors, is surmounted by a tetrahedral dome with skylight pouring in through it. The facets of the dome were painted by artists from the Moscow Armoury after Philippe Pillement's sketches in 1721. Canvases by Western European painters of the seventeenth and early eighteenth centuries decorate the walls of its interior. The paintings on display in the Lusthaus are part of the extensive Monplaisir collection, which mainly consists of works by Dutch and Flemish masters. The pictures were bought abroad on the orders of Peter the Great himself. The galleries connecting the two Lusthaus blocks with the central building of the palace were found especially suitable for the display of the paintings.

The Eastern Gallery is about twenty metres long. Sixteen glazed doors, from the floor to the ceiling, fill the interior with light and air introducing a feeling of its harmony with the surrounding scenery. There is practically no wall on the southern side and on the northern one the window apertures grew much narrower and form piers panelled with oak. The ceiling and coves are decorated with ornamental painted motifs and with the use of gold by Philippe Pillement. The medallion in the centre of the plafond features an allegory of *Summer* – a subject fashionable in the eighteenth century.

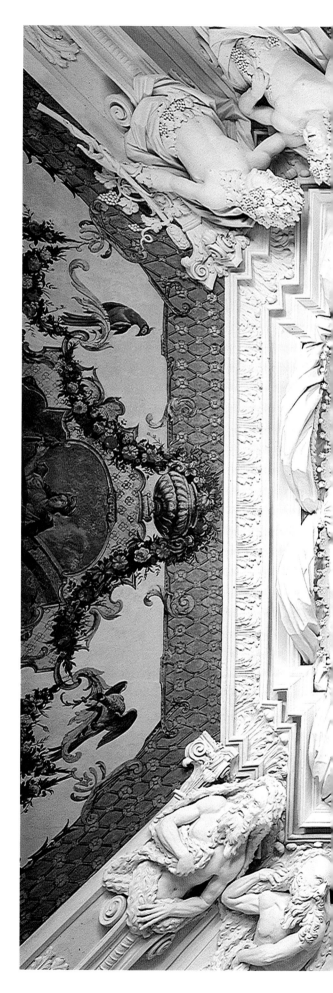

The Hall. Ph. Pillement.
The ceiling painted over stuccowork

215

The wide piers between the windows on the northern side were suitable for hanging pictures in pairs, one over another. It was, however, not by their subject-matter, artistic manner or colour scheme that the choice was made – the only thing that mattered was the size. The plain black frames of the paintings stand out clearly against the background of the warm-toned walls faced with elegantly carved oak panels. Twenty-one of the original paintings have survived. With the exception of three Italian works, represented here are pictures by Dutch and Flemish painters of the eighteenth and nineteenth centuries. This choice reflects the tastes of the Monplaisir owner. The paintings were acquired mainly at auctions in Amsterdam during Peter the Great's visits, and often painters themselves helped him to make his choice. One can hardly trace any consistent idea behind the selection of the paintings except for the Tsar's apparent liking of marines.

During the Petrine period Monplaisir housed 201 paintings. Their lot in the seaside palace was sad. Not heated in winter, exposed to strong winds and damaged by water during floods, Monplaisir is by no means an ideal art repository. There are 147 paintings on display in the palace today and 120 of them belonged to the originals collection.

Among the paintings of the Eastern Gallery one should single out two works by the Flemish painter Daniel van Heil. One of them, *The Destruction of Sodom*, was inspired by a Biblical subject and the other, *Aeneas' Flight from Troy*, was based on the poem *Aeneid* by the Roman poet Virgil. The most notable pictures in the gallery are *Falconry* by the Dutchmen Philips Wouwerman and *Calm on the Sea* by the well-known marine painter Adriaen van de Velde.

On crossing the threshold of the Lacquer Study, the visitor suddenly finds himself in the magic oriental kingdom – the walls in the room are faced with black lacquer panels set in ornate red frames. The painting on a black lacquer ground is executed in gold with figures in relief. The pictures feature landscapes, gardens, scenes of hunting and fishing, birds and plants. Fixed on the vertical strips between the panels are carved and gilt brackets with their shelves supported by putti and sirens. The shelves are used to display pieces of Oriental porcelain which found

The Hall.
A. Storck. A City Pier

The Kitchen

their way to Monplaisir in Peter's time. The ceiling painting, an allegory of *Autumn*, matches the overall subject of the palace plafonds – that of the *Seasons*. Pillement portrayed here a *Bacchante* holding a cluster of grapes and a wine-cup and symbolizing *Autumn*. The decor of this room is typical for the European palaces of the late seventeenth and early eighteenth centuries.

Work on the decoration of the Lacquer Study began to designs by Johann Braunstein in 1719 and already by February 1722 ten Russian icon-painters had completed ninety-four lacquer panels. Jean Michel and his French and Russian assistants were responsible for the woodwork.

The study had retained its original appearance until World War II. Painters from the village of Palekh, a well-known Russian centre of lacquer painting, used several undamaged panels for recreating the lost ones. The door from the Lacquer Study leads to the central interior of the palace which is known as the Hall. Its glazed doors look onto the garden and the northern ones face the sea. The formal character of the room intended for reception of guests is emphasized by its dimensions and the wealth of its decor. Its walls, like those in the galleries, are richly decorated with oak panels with paintings in black frames set into them. But the most remarkable feature of the interior is the dome-shaped tetragonal ceiling painted by Philippe Pillement. The four facets in the coving bear the images of ancient gods symbolizing the four elements – *Water*, *Air*, *Fire* and *Earth*. Above them the painter depicted allegories of winds and temperaments. *Apollo*, the god of sun, art, poetry and sunshine, reigns supreme over all this magnificence. In the corners, at the joints of the facets, are sculptural groups of half-length figures which symbolize the four seasons. These are true masterpieces of sculpture of the first quarter

The Lacquer Study

of the eighteenth century. Although one of surviving documents mentions the authorship of a French sculptor, his name has not been identified.

Among the twenty-two paintings hung in the Hall of particular interest are the representations of ships riding at anchor by Adam Silo, a painter who was also a ship-builder, a captain and an engraver. It was his versatility that attracted Peter the Great when he studied ship-building in Amsterdam. Legend has it that the Tsar used Silo's paintings to examine cadets at the Naval Academy in Russia. The fireplace shield is decorated with *A Vase of Flowers* by the Flemish artist Pieter Casteels, a large-scale painting which is a typical still life of the early eighteenth century. Among genre paintings one should pay particular attention to the subject of *Jolly*

Company by the Dutch painter Anthonie Palamedesz. Battle painting is represented by *The Siege of Tournai* by Louis XIV, the work of the French artist Adam Frans van de Meulen.

In the eighteenth century, auxiliary services were rarely located within the central part of the palace. Peter the Great, borrowing a lot of elements from Dutch houses, was attracted by such rational layout with the proximity of a kitchen to a formal hall and dwelling rooms.

The decoration of the Kitchen was finished in the summer of 1723 and soon Catherine I, the wife of Peter the Great, "prepared food herself" there. In the centre of the room stands a huge stove with a hood over it and with suspended shelves. The most noticeable feature of the room is that the walls here are covered from floor to cornice with painted tiles of fifty various subjects – landscapes with houses and animals, human figures and sailboats at sea. The blue colour of the tiling lends a special warm atmosphere and the feeling of tidyiness to the interior. The decorative tiles were brought to Russia from Delft, a Dutch town which supplied them to all of Europe. The tiles were sometimes used to embellish not only kitchens but dwelling rooms as well.

The vessels placed on the stove and shelves correspond to the designation of the Kitchen: Delft faience dishes with designs in cobalt blue, porcelain plates painted in colours which were brought from China by the Dutch East-India Company, English utensils of pewter, Russian copper cauldrons, etc.

The door from the Kitchen opens to the room where kitchen utensils and table-linen were stored. It is the only room, the walls of which are smoothly plastered. But even this interior, inspite of its purely utilitarian purpose, has some decorative features – the unusual pattern of its parquet floor, its fireplace decorated with moulding and, lastly, the majestic painted composition showing a woman with a burning brazier, an allegory of *Winter*, on its ceiling. As any pantry, it contained glassware and ceramic vessels: Dutch faience dishes and vases, Russian bottles, decanters and all sorts of goblets and wine-glasses. Standing on the fireplace are eight brown stoneware tea-pots which were, according to tradition, presented to Peter the Great by the Chinese Emperor.

To the west of the Hall are the Emperor's private apartments. His study is particularly impressive. Through the small-scale panes of its windows overlooking the sea, one could perfectly observe the fortress island of Kronstadt on the one side and St Petersburg on the other. The walls here, like in other rooms, are panelled with oak and the panels are adorned with tiles depicting thirteen types of eighteenth-century ships. The oval plafond painted by Philippe Pillement shows monkeys gamboling amidst garlands and flowers.

Peter the Great liked this room. By lifting the lower half of the window he could watch ships passing by to the northern capital of Russian and to the west. The old instruments kept in a sideboard remind us of the Emperor's nautical activities. Above them one can see a steel casket presented to Peter the Great by Tula craftsmen.

The paintings hanging in the Naval Study deserve special mention. These include ten landscapes by Frans de Paula Ferg, three works based on ancient subjects by Victor Janssens and, as usual, depictions of piers. One of such pictures belongs to the brush of

The Lacquer Study.
Shelves with porcelain pieces

The Pantry. Ph. Pillement.
The ceiling painted
over stuccowork

Hendrik van der Moon, a Dutch painter of the first half of the seventeenth century.

The Bedroom is adjacent to the Maritime Study. Originally its walls were lined with Dutch green cloth, but already in the 1830s the worn-out lining was removed. Now it has been replaced by olive-coloured woollen fabric which perfectly harmonizes with the oak doors and the tracery of the windows. A particular air of festivity is lent to the interior by its fireplace the shield of which is decorated with an amazingly elaborate moulded pattern. In the centre of the room stands a huge bed with a canopy over it and next to it is a table-top brazier executed in the eighteenth century by Spanish craftsmen from the town of Pamplona. The wooden mug with a set of glasses and a salt-cellar put inside was made and painted by master-craftmen from Archangel. The jug and the tub for washing, coated in black lacquer, are of English work. All these objects were Peter the Great's personal belongings.

While Peter the Great stayed in Monplaisir, the room located to the south from the Bedroom was occupied by his batman. However, as to its decor, the interior shows no major difference from that in the owner's apartments. The walls here are panelled as elsewhere; the room has an inlaid floor and a moulded fireplace, and its ceiling is painted with Bacchic scenes and ornaments. As regards the quality and number of paintings, the Secretary's Room, which has twenty-four pictures, is even richer than the Emperor's study. The two marines painted on panels in grisaille by Adriaen van der Salm are notable among them. They portray ships at roadstead near Archangel and Amsterdam and serve as an evidence of long-standing links between these two port cities.

The design of the the Western Gallery and the Lusthaus is absolutely identical with that of their counterparts in the eastern wing of the palace. The painted plafond and the pictures play the major part in the decor of this interior. The choice and character of the paintings in the gallery and Lusthaus are similar to those in the other rooms of the palace – they are decorated with works by Adam Silo and other masters. The two views of Zandaam, a town in Holland where Peter the Great lived and worked, painted by Frans van der Horn, are noteworthy among them.

Already during the reconstruction of the Dutch House it became obvious that its dimensions could not provide accomodation even for the narrow circle of close associates and relatives of the Tsar. In 1719 Johann Braunstein began to erect, perpendicular to the Palace, two galleries, or "Family Apartments", which were completed a year later.

Both galleries had four sets of rooms each having a separate entrance and consisting of a vestibule and two rooms. Inside the rooms were plastered and whitewashed. In 1721 Peter the Great

The Bedroom.
Toilet set
of Peter the Great

ordered that they be provided with corner fireplaces, which have survived to the present day. Braunstein linked the galleries with the two lusthaus pavilions by arches with semicircular tops. Stylistically, the galleries draw on Monplaisir and therefore they blend completely with the architectural ensemble. The "Family Apartments" were intended for those who came to stay at Peterhof. In 1724, Peter the Great compiled special "Rules" regulating the behavour of his guests there.

The Bedroom.
G. Dou. Food Shop

The Bedroom ▶

$\mathcal{D}$uring Monplaisir's early period vegetables used to be grown opposite the auxiliary structures within the western limits of the garden and then a small stone orangery was built on the site. In 1748–49 Rastrelli used its foundations with an undercroft to erect a new stone palace, larger than the Dutch House, for Elizabeth Petrovna. The main façade of this palace looked onto the Monplasir Garden and had a porch with its door leading to the Lower Park. The decoration of the palace took a long time and was finished only in the 1750s.

The Baroque interior of the Elizabethan Palace existed for a little more than thirty years. Already in 1785–86 it was completely altered (except for the parquet design and the tiled stoves in some rooms) by the Italian architect Giacomo Quarenghi, an Italian architect invited to Russia by Catherine the Great. As a result the smooth colouring of the walls, the pilasters and the snow-white reliefs replaced the whimsical gilt carvings, the shine of mirrors and the bright fabrics.

The first decades of the nineteenth century saw some more refashioning of the interiors. In several rooms, the ceilings and the coves were decorated with paintings in the Empire style. The work has been ascribed to Giovanni Scotti.

Before World War II the Catherine Block stood next to the wooden galleries originally intended for the "Hill Palaces" (the future Great Palace). Not used there, they were erected to Rastrelli's design near the Peter's orangery and after the construction of the Catherine Block were linked with the latter by a special passage.

In this wooden wing there were the private apartments of Catherine II, then Grand Duchess Yekaterina Alexeyevna, in which she lived for fifteen years at the court of Elizabeth. It was from here that she made her first steps to glory. On 28 June 1762 the wife of the Russian Emperor Peter III left her Peterhof house to come back a day after the coup d'état, accompanied by the Guards as the Empress, and to win later the name of Catherine the Great.

Catherine recollected about this event in her Memoirs: "I slept quietly at Peterhof, and at 6:28 in the morning Alexei Orlov entered my room and said:

The Green Reception Room

'It is time to get up – everything is ready to proclaim you.' I took a seat in a carriage. We went to the Izmailovsky Regiment... Soldiers gathered, kissed me... and they began to take the oath." In commemoration of this event the palace was named the Catherine Block. It was used for formal dinners and annual balls of the graduates of the Smolny Institute for Girls of Noble Birth inaugurated by Catherine II in St Petersburg in 1764.

The Green Reception Room is the first of the eight rooms in the Catherine Block, to which visitors proceed from Peter's guest gallery, owes its name to the colour of its walls. The main decorative elements are similar in the majority of the rooms – the classical mouldings, the Empire-style painting in grisaille, the single-tone colouring of the walls and the smooth ceiling, sometimes with a rosette in the centre.

All these decorative features are present in the decoration of the Golden Reception Room: the coves are embellished with griffins, lyres, armorial trophies, banners, etc.; the frieze is made up of elegant moulded rosettes, while the walls are adorned with round wreaths of almost naturalistically rendered flowers and fruit. Scotti's painted decor which was added, in the 1800s, to the mouldings surviving from the time of Quarenghi has changed the subject-matter of the interior decoration. Fasces, swords and helmets gave an official air to the Green Reception Room. The huge marble fireplace brought from Italy was installed in the room to the design of Quarenghi.

The Empire-style painting of the room organically blends with the splendid furniture of poplar with carved and gilt trimmings, produced in St Petersburg to the design of the outstanding architect Carlo Rossi. This set of furniture has never left Peterhof.

The artistic bronzework in the collection of the Catherine Block is represented mainly by French pieces from the late eighteenth and early nineteenth centuries. Of particular interest are the clock *Apollo's Chariot* made by the famous French bronzeworker Pierre-Philippe Thomire after the drawing of Jean-Demosthène Dugoure

The Bedroom of Alexander I

The Green Reception Room.
Furniture set.
After a drawing by C. Rossi.
Russia. 1810s

and the companion tripod bowls from the workshop of the same master-craftsman. The bronze censer on the table before the sofa is a work by the St Petersburg craftsman de Lancris.

The two westward-looking rooms are traditionally associated with Alexander I's stay in Peterhof. This Emperor spent a large part of his reign outside Russia, in military campaigns and foreign travels.

Everything in the Study reminds the visitor of the heroic years of Russia's war against Napoleon's army – the bas-reliefs after models by Fiodor Tolstoi, the paper-weight made of cannon-balls from the Borodino Battlefield, the obelisk in honour of the victory over the enemy's forces, and the cabinet with cups and goblets decorated with portraits of the heroes of the 1812 Patriotic War.

Under the portrait of Paul I, on the bureau produced by the famous German cabinet-maker Heinrich Gambs who worked for the Russian court, there are two small incense vases of jasper and rhodonite. They were manufactured about 1811 at the Ekaterinburg Lapidary Factory and presented to Alexander I by Count Pavel Stroganov. The bookcase containing a small library is decorated with gilt bronze busts of the Emperor and his wife, Yelizaveta Alexeyevna, and the corner cabinets are adorned with porcelain vases from the study of Alexander I in the Anichkov Palace in St Petersburg.

The central feature of the Bedroom of Alexander I is the mahogany state bed, known as *ladya* (boat). By the head of the bed are candelabra of gilt and patinated bronze by the famous French bronzeworker Lenoir Ravrio. Nearby is a table with a *solitaire* tea service manufactured at the Imperial Porcelain Factory in St Petersburg in the early nineteenth century.

Although Alexander did not pay long visits to Peterhof, the summer residence was enriched with new fountains during his reign. At that time the famous Peterhof festivities were inaugurated, which were described in many works of literature and later became traditional. But perhaps the most important mark left at Peterhof by the twenty-year reign of Catherine the Great's grandson is the sizeable addition to the palatial collections of art objects. These included his father's acquisitions in Europe, ambassadorial gifts and private presents. Of note among the bronzework are the objects bought for the Mikhailovsky Palace in 1801 and transferred to Peterhof

The Blue Reception Room

230

after the death of Paul I, the owner of the palace, on the orders of
his son. These are two censers of gilt bronze with pedestals of green
marble, the statues of *Zephyr* and *Flora* and two jugs by the foot
of the bed.

The visitor's attention is attracted by a painting on the northern wall. It is *A Young Shepherd Surprised by a Storm* (1810) by the
English painter George Dawe and the painting *Diana and Endy-
mion* by the Swiss painter Angelica Kauffmann.

The Heating Room is the only interior in the palace preserv-
ing Rastrelli's decoration without any alterations. The kitchen "in
the Dutch manner" was designed here for Elizabeth Petrovna, the
daughter of Peter the Great, in 1760. The focal centre of the room
is a huge whitewashed stove with twelve cooking rings and a large
oven. Legend has it that in this kitchen the Empress cooked herself "her meals, not rarely inventing absolutely new dishes". In the
corner of the room, in the lobby, is a staircase leading to an extensive basement from where the stove was stoken.

On display in the show-cases flanking the entrance to the
Anteroom are items from palatial dinner services produced as commissions for the Imperial court. Two
of them are particularly notable: the Ropsha Service (its name derives from the Ropsha Palace
in the neighbourhood of Peterhof where it
was used), and the Babigon Service, which
was employed in the Belvedere Palace at
Babigon Hill, also not far from the summer

residence. All dessert plates of the service had representations of the landmarks of Peterhof.

In the past, the outer door of the Anteroom was used as an entrance to the Catherine Block. The decor of this room reflects all the three stages in the construction of the building. Thus, its tiled stove of the mid-eighteenth century stands alongside Quarenghi's Classical fireplace. The mouldings on the walls and ceiling made to his design can be seen next to the Empire decoration of the coves and frieze with painted trophies, lyres, helmets and a representation of the goddess of victory putting a wreath on the altar.

The furnishings in the Anteroom, though seemingly united by the same kind of decor – French lacquerwork with gilt relief details – are nevertheless by different craftsmen of the first quarter of the nineteenth century who worked in keeping with the projects of the leading architects of Russia. Among the latter were Andrei Voronikhin, Carlo Rossi and Luigi Rusca. The two console tables standing by the walls, with carved and gilt bases and with ancient mosaics on their table-tops, came to Russia in the late eighteenth century through the agency of Nikolai Demidov, the Russian envoy to Florence.

The decor of this small room, the Corner Reception Room, at one time used as a passage to the wooden galleries which then adjoined the stone block, is rather modest. Its another name, "Paul's Reception Room", is perhaps connected with recollections of the years Grand Duchess Yekaterina Alexeyevna spent here with her son. Some interesting details to the atmosphere of the period are added by the personal belongings of the Empress, her hus-

G. Dawe. Portrait of Empreror
Alexander I. 1825

band Peter III and their son Paul Petrovich, later Emperor Paul I, who was murdered in the Mikhailovsky Palace in St Petersburg. A true embellishment of this room is a beautiful furniture set veneered with poplar. It was produced in the 1810s to the design of the famous Russian architect Vasily Stasov specially for Peterhof.

The Blue Reception Room derives its name from the colour of its walls. All the furniture of the Blue Reception Room was created in Russia. Of greatest interest are the two chests of drawers produced in the 1790s and decorated with grisaille scenes from Virgil's *Aeneid*. The piano made at the Johann A. Tischner Factory in St Petersburg recalls the concerts given to the Imperial family and its guests in the eighteenth and nineteenth centuries.

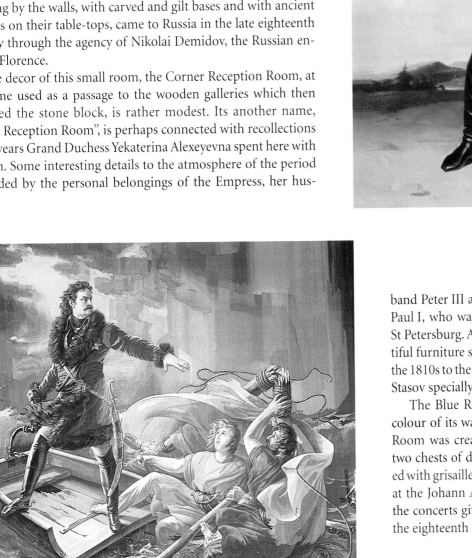

The Yellow Hall .
Tapestry. Paris. Early 19th century

233

The huge Yellow Hall with its exquisite Classical decor by Quarenghi is the main interior of the Catherine Block. Its walls are divided by sixteen paired pilasters of the Corinthian order; between them are grotesque stucco mouldings including a classical vase, plant shoots, bowls and a female figure in an oval medallion; over the four doors of the Hall are the bas-reliefs by the sculptor Jean-Dominique Rachette glorifying architecture, music, theatre and science in allegorical form. The interior is lit by seven beautiful chandeliers made of gilt wood and putty by Russian craftsmen in the early twentieth century.

The gobelin embroidered at the famous Paris Factory in the early nineteenth century after a painting by Charles Steuben is devoted to a memorable historical episode. It shows Peter the Great rescuing fishermen during a storm on Lake Ladoga. The gobelin was commissioned by Napoleon I, but was finished in the reign of Louis XVIII who presented it to Alexander I.

The walls of the hall are also adorned with portraits of the Russian Emperors: an early-nineteenth-century copy from a portrait of Catherine the Great by Johann-Baptist Lampi the Elder, and a portrait of Alexander I painted by George Dawe in 1825. The clock by Pierre-Philippe Thomire placed under Alexander I's portrait repeats the famous sculptural composition of the monument to Minin and Pozharsky on Red Square in Moscow.

The best decoration of the Yellow Hall is the Guryev Service, the most magnificent among Russian porcelain services. It was named after Count Dmitry Guryev who commissioned the set at the Imperial Porcelain Factory in St Petersburg for the Imperial court. Its original name, the "Russian Service", exactly reflects the subject of its decor. It is a sort of encyclopaedia of Russian life. Its plates contained representations of dozens of various folk types illustrating the population of the huge country, and a wine-cooler bore views of St Petersburg and its environs, as well as sights of Moscow. The painters who

The Yellow Hall. The Guryev Service.
The Imperial Porcelain Factory,
St Petersburg. 1809–17

235

decorated the service drew on Johann Georgi's book *The Peoples of Russia* and Christian Gottfried Geissler's *St Petersburg Scenes and Types* as well as paintings by Mikhail Vorobyov, Fiodor Alexeyev and Semion Shchedrin. Three-dimensional objects were adorned with sculptures of young boys and girls wearing Russian national costumes. They were designed by the sculptor Stepan Pimenov. The

war against Napoleon's France delayed the creation of the service until 1817. Originally it was intended for 50 persons, but later the number was supplemented several times and towards the end of the nineteenth century the set included about 500 items. The brilliance of this service was emphasized by crystal items commissioned in England by Paul I in the late eighteenth century.

View of the Bathhouse Block from
the Chinese Garden

THE CHINESE GARDEN

A small Chinese garden in the so-called landscape style adjoins the Monplaisir complex from the east, from the gulf side. The garden was designed by the architect Eduard Hahn in 1866. The creators of such gardens aimed at reaching the maximum variety of landscape scenery. To enliven the flat relief of the area, a hillock was raised there. Mounted on its top is a marble sculptural group, *Cupid and Psyche*, a copy of Canova's original. This spot affords a splendid view of the gulf. On the northern slope of the hillock is a tufa grotto with two marble stepways shaped as shells. The brook running from the grotto streams down the edges of the shells and feeds water to the small pond which has a tufa island with a fountain jet in the centre of it. The structure is known as the Shell Cascade. The clusters of trees, the small brook with humpbacked bridges spanning it, the marble statues, the winding walks and the flower-beds, all adds to the special air of cosiness and splendour characteristic of the Chinese Garden.

The Chinese garden. The Shell Cascade ▶
Cupid and Psyche. Copy of Canova's original

238

THE BATH HOUSE

*A*ttached to the eastern wing from the side of the Monplaisir Garden is a single-storey building with a tent-shaped hipped roof. This is the so-called Bath House. Originally, the Monplaisir estate included, among other household structures, bathing pools and baths built in 1721–22. In 1748, instead of Peter's small wooden bath house, a new one, also in wood, was erected there and a crystal bath inserted into a copper casing was installed. In 1765, the construction of a swimming pool with a lifting bottom and an inlet of sea water began. Unsalted water was fed from the Moujichok (Peasant) Fountain in the centre of the pool. The work was finished only in the 1770s when pipes were laid along the perimeter of the octagonal pool inside with water-jets spouting from them. Later, already in 1800, the Moujichok was replaced by a tall gilt column with water-thrusting sphere on top. In addition to the room containing a bathing-pool and a shower-bath, the Bath House had cold-water bathrooms and a Russian steam-bath, as well as the Toilet Room and the Entrance Room.

In 1865–66 the old wooden wing was replaced by a new stone building erected to the design of the architect Eduard Hahn. Redesigning the building he tried to retain the eighteenth-century style – he even simply imitated the architecture of Monplaisir. However, the evident lack of integrity in the design of the façades

The Cold Bathroom ▶

240

N. Tiutriumov. A Reposing Bacchante

and the apparent overloading with details betray a nineteenth-century builder. Nevertheless, the architect left intact the original layout of the building, the bathing-pool with a fountain and the steambath. The Bath House had retained such an appearance until World War II. In 1997 a museum of the history of daily life was opened there.

The Reception Room – the small room with a single window overlooking the Monplaisir Garden is remarkable for its simple decor. When an Empress took a bath or shower, her maid of honour was waiting upon her.

The paintings hung in the room emphasize its private character. The Reception Room displays the painting *A Soubrette* by the French artist Emile-Antoine Bayard, who turned in his creative quests to the world of the theatre. The Dutch marine painter Hermanus Koekkoek was one of those painters whose works were readily bought by contemporaries. His *Seascape* decorating the wall

of the Reception Room executed in the best traditions of the Old Dutch Masters. In the second half of the nineteenth century it was fashionable to decorate interiors not only with paintings, but with sculptures too. The Reception Room is adorned with the bronze statue *Crying Satyr* by Michel Claudion, an artist active in Rome for a long time and carrying out commissions of dignitaries and royal persons including Catherine the Great.

After treatment the Empress relaxed in the Dressing-Room, drank coffee or tea; sometimes small parties of people closest to her were held there. The walls and ceiling are lined with blue calico, and over it with white muslin in gathers. A set of soft gilt furniture in the Second Rococo style, upholstered with cloth bearing a blue plant ornament and consisting of armchairs, chairs and a sofa, perfectly blends with the decor of the interior. The painting *A Scene at the Harpsichord* by the Italian painter Francesco Vinea hangs over the sofa.

The rocaille motifs are also used to decorate the articles of Russian porcelain made at the Imperial Porcelain Factory and at the Miklashevsky Factory in the nineteenth century – scent bottles, soap-boxes, powder-cases and other female toilet items. They are standing on a dressing table near a mirror, which is draped with a tulle cover embellished by an applique work in keeping with the fashion of the period.

On the tea table stands a silver tray with a silver-plated samovar. It was made at the F. Dubinin Factory founded in St Petersburg in the 1840s. The teapot, coffee-pot and sugar bowl, also in silver, produced at the Fraget Factory in Poland, make up a single set with the samovar, as do the porcelain cup and saucer adorned with cobalt blue and polychrome painting, made at the Kornilov Factory in the 1840s.

The Cold Bathroom occupies the central part of the Bathhouse Block. It is the most imposing interior of the palace with a dome-shaped ceiling and a wide cove decorated at the corners by an ornamental painting in grisaille. Under the cornice, along the perimeter of the building, are located forty moulded consoles.

The Cold Bathroom. Shower in the form of chandelier

The Warm Bathroom

The fireplaces are also adorned with moulded Baroque rocailles. The walls of the Cold Bathroom are adorned with genre paintings popular during the period of Eclecticism – two canvases by Gottfried Willewalde, *An Arch* and *A Soldier's Visit*, as well as the picture *A Cavalcade in a Forest* by the German painter F.-V. Pfeiffer.

In the centre of the room stands a polished oak bathtub with its bottom sunk below the floor level and provided with steps and rails of turned balusters to enter it. Over the bath hangs a chandelier with a gilt net for a shower adorned with glass leaves, vine grapes and decorative glazed candlesticks shaped like bindweed flowers. It was bought for Maria Alexandrovna from the St Petersburg bronzesmith Diepner in the nineteenth century. Lost during the war, the chandelier was recreated from three surviving fragments of the glass, pre-war photographs, archive materials and analogous chandelier surviving in the Voltaire Room in the Sans-Souci Palace at Potsdam.

In the Warm Bathroom behind a screen in the niche stands a marble bath fixed on the floor, a work by Alessandro Triscorni. Over it are two taps, for hot and cold water. Behind the small door of the closet was placed a tank for hot water supplied to the bath through a pipe. The intimate character of the interior is emphasized by the painting *A Reposing Bacchante* by Nikanor Tiutriumov, an artist who painted the figures of nude beauties with a great mastery.

Hung over the bath are porcelain plaques in frames with overglaze polychrome painted decoration – copies from pictures by

Clock: A Bather

Philippe Wouwermann. These works were produced by the masters of figure painting Alexander Mironov, Timofei Semionov and Alexei Stoletov at the Imperial Porcelain Factory in the 1850s and 1860s. On the shelves of the cupboard are a porcelain soap-box, a wash-basin and a jug covered with cobalt blue under a glaze and painted in gold and silver, as well as two *bourdaloues* or bed-pans. They owe their name to Louis Bourdaloue, one of the most eloquent French orators in the age of Louis XIV. Bourdaloue's carefully reasoned and uncompromising sermons had a great success. He often preached at the court and court ladies, in order not to miss a single word from his fiery long speeches, took special vessels with them hiding them in their muffs.

In the nineteenth century all Emperors and Empresses used to attend the Steam Bath.

In the corner of the Steam Bathroom stands a tiled stove with copper doors and a metal sheet on which 108 cannonballs 0.5 inch in diameter are placed. The idea to replace traditional stones used for heating a steam bath with cast-iron cannonballs was evolved at Peterhof during the age of Peter the Great. When water was poured onto red-hot stones they often cracked, whereas the cannonballs were durable.

E.-A. Bayard. A Soubrette

The Steam Bathroom ▶

THE ASSEMBLY HALL

he Assembly Hall is located behind the Bathhouse Block. In the eighteenth century this interior was known as the "hall where cavaliers dine" or the "Moorish Hall" – the name "Assembly Hall" would appear later. The walls are lined with oak-wood and decorated with seventeen tapestries woven in the first half of the eighteenth century at the St Petersburg Tapestry Factory. Eight large thematic tapestries had conventional names after the parts o the world – *Africa*, *Asia* and *America* – and represented landscapes with dark-skinned inhabitants of these countries, exotic vegetables, wild beasts, fishes and birds. Russian craftsmen reproduced the subjects of "Indian tapestries" woven in France after cartoons by the artist Alexandre-François

Desportes and presented to Peter the Great in 1717. The piers between the windows are adorned with nine narrow tapestries woven after cartoons of Philippe Pillement, with ornamental compositions including images of zephyrs, baskets of flowers and *commedia dell'arte* characters.

The so-called Everyday Service exhibited on the table in the Assembly Hall was made at the Imperial Porcelain Factory in the late eighteenth and early nineteenth centuries and was used for usual dinners. It is adorned with decorative patterns in the shape of bouquets of flowers and includes all kinds of dinner and dessert plates, tureens, wine coolers, an ice-cream bowl, vases for berries and fruit, etc.

*The Assembly Hall
Tapestry: America*

THE KITCHEN

he Assembly Hall adjoins the Pantry intended for storing things necessary for serving imperial tables: table linen, utensils and vessels, and the Kitchen, whose windows afford a beautiful view of the Lower Park. Opposite its windows a brick vault stretches along the walls. It consists of four tent-shaped ventilating hoods for collecting and removing smokes, smells and steams during the preparation of food. Under the tent-shaped hoods are stoves, and near the entrance to the Coffee-Room stands a Russian-type stove. The Kitchen created after a design by Francesco Bartolomeo Rossi in the middle of the eighteenth century functioned until the early twentieth century. During the Sec-

ond World War the southern wall of the Kitchen suffered from an explosion. During the restoration of the floor made from Rastrelli's drawings, authentic eighteenth-century bricks were used. They were taken from the bottom of the Gulf of Finland where they had been stored during reconstruction work or demolition of some Peterhof structures.

The Kitchen, as a place where exquisite dishes for the imperial court were cooked. Near the entrance to the Pantry stands a table for kneading and rolling out dough on which scoops for flour are displayed. A tool for chopping sugar can be seen on the wall nearby. On the floor are barrels for beer and kvass, and on the shelves of the cupboard are various moulds for cakes, jellies and mousses, a hand-beater, an ice-cream bowl, a mortar with pestle and glass fly-traps for catching flies by sweetened water. On the upper shelf are silver wine and water coolers made at the St Petersburg and Moscow factories in the second half of the nineteenth century. Palatial tableware of earlier times is also on display here. Over the table are pewter plates commissioned by Peter the Great in England in the 1720s. Tin, a soft silvery metal, highly valued in Russia, was used for the production of table utensils and vessels. Along the walls stand tables used to prepare products for cooking. Steelyards and scales for weighing food hang on a metal cross-piece fixed between the windows. Hot dishes could be prepared at the Monplaisir Kitchen in several ways: in the Russian stove, on a trivet, on skewers and on a cooking stove. In the central part of the Kitchen stand two cooking stoves. One of them has a copper fish-steamer with a grated insert for preparing fish over steam; on the other are two boilers for water. Nearby is a confectioner's stove where basins for cooking jams, a tub and a waffle-

*Set of forks,
knives and spoons
with porcelain hafts*

Carafe for four kinds of wine

iron used for baking waffles and gingerbread can be seen. The confectioner prepared fruit and berry jellies, biscuits, sweets, candied fruit and other sweetmeats. Behind this cooking stove is the Russian stove faced inside with fire-brick. Next to it are oven-forks for cast-iron cauldrons and shovels for bread baked on metal sheets. Copper vessels, tinned inside to prevent them from oxidation, were preferred for cooking food at the Kitchen. On the shelves of the kitchen are examples of Russian copper vessels dating from the seventeenth to nineteenth century: *endovas* (large containers for drinks), loving cups, ladles, casseroles, etc.

In the Coffee-Room is a collection of diverse nineteenth-century samovars made in the shape of vases or urns, as well as pear-, ball- or egg-shaped varieties. The body of the samovar was divided by rocaille or lobate decorations, adorned with stylized geometrical motifs or overlaid details in the form of leaves, flower buds, etc.

Special vessels for brewing and drinking tea and coffee were used. Displayed in the cupboard of the Coffee-Room is a porcelain service of the late nineteenth – early twentieth century made at the Imperial Porcelain Factory and decorated with a flower ornament over a blue field. It includes cups with saucers for tea and coffee, a milk-jar, a teapot, a coffee-pot and other items. The Coffee-Room shows objects necessary for preparing coffee: a brazier dating from the second half of the nineteenth century, coffee-grinders, coffee-makers and a coffee-pot, all made of brass. Hot chocolate was not as popular at the Russian court as coffee. It was considered a delicacy and was served on birthday or name-day celebrations of some member of the imperial family.

*View of the Russian-style stove
and the confectioner's stove*

Copper vessels

J. Gillemans. ▶
Still Life with Lobster

THE MUSEUM
OF ART COLLECTORS

The Upper Gardens Mansion, situated in the eastern part of the Upper Gardens, houses the Museum of Art Collectors which displays the collections and individual objects presented to the Peterhof Museum Complex. The main part of the display is occupied by the four collections bequeathed to Peterhof by the inhabitants of St Petersburg, Iosif Ezrakh and Roza Timofeyeva as well as the Muscovites I. Kavarskaya and A. Usenina. A separate room is allotted to changing exhibitions of the graphic works presented to the museum by the art collector Yury Varshavsky. The museum's stocks and restoration workshops occupy the upper and basement floors.

Solitaire. Porcelain Factory,
Höchst, Germany. Ca 1770

The well traceable history of the construction of the Upper Gardens Mansion was closely connected with the life of the court. In 1754 Rastrelli was completing the redesigning of the Upper Chambers and simultaneously began the erection of the new monumental railing around the Upper Gardens. At the same time at its western and eastern borders were constructed one-storey stone kitchens. The building at the eastern line of the Upper Gardens – at the site of the future Upper Gardens Mansion – was occupied by the so-called First Stone Kitchen, a one-storey building with its front facing Dvortsovaya (Palace) Street. In 1843–47 the architect Joseph Charlemagne redesigned the First Kitchen and turned it into a three-storey building that survives. In 1861 the First Kitchen was transferred to the New Waiters' House and the former building, as is said in the decree, "was to be accommodated for a sojourn of cavaliers". The building was reconstructed according to a project by Nikolai Benois only in 1867–69. In keeping with this plan the rooms of the ground floor were intended for the residence of sixty policemen and the middle and upper ones consisted of flats provided with all necessary furniture. Thus the First Kitchen was transformed into the Cavaliers' Mansion in

V. Shukhayev. Portrait of the Actress A. Heinz. 1916–17

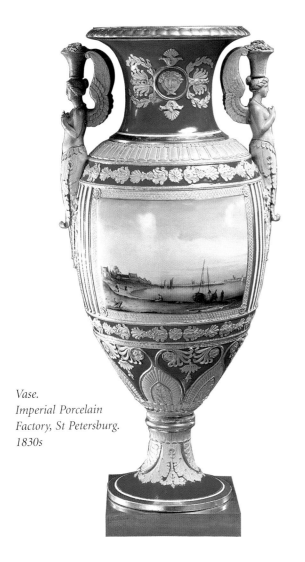

Vase.
Imperial Porcelain
Factory, St Petersburg.
1830s

the Upper Gardens. In summertime the Chief Marshal of the Imperial Court Count A. Shuvalov, the confessor of their Majesties V. Bazhanov and the Minister of the Imperial Household Baron V. Frederiks used to live in these apartments.

After the Revolution of 1917 the Ministerial Mansion, as it was then called, housed the first committee of the Petrodvorets Komsomol (Young Communist League) and after the War of 1941–45 the building was first used for dwelling and then stayed unoccupied for a long time.

The very layout of the building with the suite system of rooms that was transferred to the disposal of the museum-preserve suggested the creation of a museum in it. After restoration work the Museum of Art Collectors has opened for visitors in 2002.

THE BENOIS FAMILY MUSEUM

Not far from the Great Palace, on the south-eastern border of the square in front of the Church Block, there stand two similar two-storey buildings, known as the Maids-of-Honour Blocks. They were built to the plans of Nikolai Benois, Court Architect to Emperor Nicholas I, in 1858. The decor of the façades, apparently modelled on eighteenth-century examples, was explained by the proximity of Rastrelli's Great Palace. The Maids-of-Honour Blocks were intended for the accommodation of those members of the court who accompanied the Imperial family to Peterhof for the summers.

In 1988 one of the blocks was converted into a museum of the Benois family. It occupies a special place in the complex of the Pe-terhof museums. Louis Jules Benois, a confectioner, came to Russia in 1794. Starting from his son, Nicolas Benois, who became a prom-inent architect, the family took an active part in the artistic life of St Petersburg. The museum is unique even among artistic collections of the country. Amassed there are works by several generations of one family, but its artistic scope was so great that visitors to the museum have a rare opportunity to acquaint themselves with an extremely wide range of Russian and European cultural phenome-na from the nineteenth and twentieth centuries.

The members of the Benois family contributed to a wide vari-ety of arts – architecture, graphic art, theatrical design, sculpture, painting, cinema, music and literature.

A. Benois.
The Lion Cascade.
1900

A. Benois.
The Maids-of-Honour Blocks. 1900

J. Meyer. The Tsarina's Pavilion
in the Colonists' Park. Ca 1850

THE COLONISTS' PARK

In 1837–38, by a decree of Nicholas I, excavations were carried out to the south of the Upper Gardens, on the territory of the "hunters' marsh". The so-called Colonists' Park with Olga's Pond having two islets, the Tsarina's and Olga's Island, were laid out.

In 1842–44, using the design of Andrei Stakenschneider, a one-storey pavilion modelled on Pompean villas, with a tower reminiscent of an ancient house, was built. The building consisted of several rooms – a dining-room, a hall, a room containing a pool and the Empress's study. Everything in its appearance – the mosaic floor, the paintings on the walls and the statuary – reminded of the ancient Pompeian dwelling house. The Tsarina's Pavilion was a fine example of a small-scale park structure that perfectly blended with decorative sculpture and the natural environment. Such pavilions decorated the park and at the same time served for repose during walks as well as for tea-drinking in the bosom of the family.

In 1847, the architect Andrei Stakenschneider built for the daughter of Nicholas I, Grand Duchess Olga Nikolayevna who would become the Queen of Württemberg, the so-called Olga's Pavilion. This three-storey building was reminiscent of an Italian villa. Each storey consisted of a single room and had a balcony. There was an open terrace above the upper floor and a comfortable staircase led from the ground floor to the lake. The pavilion was designed in a rational and up-to-date fashion; it was encircled with greenery and adorned with decorative sculpture. Olga's Island used to be the venue of open-air performances, boating parties on the pond and illuminations.

Towering to the south-east of Olga's Pond is the Cathedral of the SS Apostles Peter and Paul erected by Nikolai Sultanov in 1905 in the so-called "Russian" style.

The Cathedral of the SS Apostles
Peter and Paul. Designed by N. Sultanov. 1905

$\mathcal{A}$LEXANDRIA

The palace and park complex of Alexandria created at Peterhof in the second quarter of the nineteenth century by eminent Western European and Russian masters is unique both as regards its eventful history and an extraordinary wealth of its architectural and artistic decoration.

The landscaped park of Alexandria, located on the shore of the Gulf of Finland to the east of the Lower Park, occupies an area of 115 hectares.

In the eighteenth century these lands belonged to Peter the Great's closest associates including Prince Alexander Menshikov and later the Princes Dolgoruky. During the reign of Anna Ioannovna the area was employed as the royal Jagdgarten or hunting ground.

In 1825 Emperor Alexander I presented this tract of land to his younger brother, Grand Duke Nikolai Pavlovich, for building a house for summer rest. Nicholas I presented the area of the former Hunting Park to his wife, the Prussian Princess Charlotte, who was named Alexandra Fiodorovna after her conversion to the Orthodox Church and marriage. The park was called "Alexandria" in her honour.

Alexandria was created under the supervision of the architects Adam Menelaws, Joseph Charlemagne, Andrei Stakenschneider and Eduard Gahn, the master gardeners Friedrich Wendelsdorf and Peter Ehrler. To make the territory more picturesque, extensive earthworks were undertaken. A great variety of trees and bushes were brought from the Botanical and Tauride Gardens in St Petersburg, from Moscow, Marseilles and Hamburg. They were skillfully arranged in matching decorative roups.

The shadowy groves and sunlit glades, hills and smooth ponds, mysterious thickets, a network of roads and paths, suddenly opening vistas of the sea, the ruins of old structures, small bridges, summerhouses and benches – all this turned Alexandria into a magnificent park reminiscent of the age of Romanticism.

◀ *The Church of St Alexander Nevsky*
(the Gothic Chapel).
Architects K. F. Schinkel, A. Menelaws
and J. Charlemagne

E. Hau. Interior of the Gothic Chapel.
Watercolour. 1840s

THE GOTHIC CHAPEL

In 1829, after the building of the Cottage Palace had been completed, there arose a necessity to build a domestic church. The place for the future chapel was chosen by Nicholas I in the western part of Alexandria. He commissioned a design of the church from Karl-Friedrich Schinkel, a major nineteenth-century German architect. The construction of the church began in 1830 under the supervision of Adam Menelaws who was succeeded by Joseph Charlemagne. In the summer of 1834 the construction work was finished and on 3 July the church was consecrated to Grand Prince St Alexander Nevsky. The church has been commonly known as the Gothic Chapel because of its distinctly medieval architectural design.

H.-P. Blanchard. The Farm Palace. 1858

THE FARM

In 1828–30, Adam Menelaws built a single-storey structure in a "rural" style, the Farm, not far from the Gothic Chapel. It had rooms for shepherds, kitchens, storerooms, and in its cattle-yard were kept pedigree cows and bulls (they were later moved to the New Farm built in 1853–54 by Stakenschneider near the highway). The eastern "pavilion" of the Farm was intended for the heir to the throne Alexander Nikolayevich. Between 1838 and 1859 Andrei Stakenschneider redesigned the Farm into the extensive two-storey Farm Palace of Emperor Alexander II and his family. The façades and interiors of the palace were fashioned in the Neo-Gothic style. Various structures required for studies or games of the grand dukes – a toy fortress, a fire observation tower, a water mill, a peasant hut and a small children's farm – emerged all around. During the Second World War the interior decor of the Farm Palace was destroyed.

The Ruin Bridge. ▶
Architect A. Menelaws. 1827–29

*A*n important landmark on the seashore was the latest major building of Alexandria – the Lower Dacha of Nicholas II, the last Russian Emperor. In 1883–85 Anton Tomishko put up a small seaside dacha with a tall stone tower and in 1895–97 he rebuilt it into an ornate and majestic summer palace with a complex of auxiliary structures. The interiors of the palace were adorned in the Art Nouveau style. The last Russian Emperor and his family spent every summer in it. Two of Nicholas's daughters, Maria and Anastasia, and his son Alexis, heir to the throne, were born. The palace was destroyed during the Second World War.

*A. Tomishko. Project for the reconstruction
of the Lower Dacha. Watercolour. 1895–97*

THE CRYSTAL COLUMN

The «Crystal» Column near the Cottage Palace. It was presented by Frederick William IV of Prussia to Empress Alexandra Fiodorovna and Emperor Nicholas I in 1854. At the present time the column is located near the Cottage Palace and after the end of restoration work it will occupy its place near the Tsarina's Pavilion.

The Crystal Column near the Cottage

*J. Meyer. The Palace at Alexandria
near Peterhof. 1840s*

THE COTTAGE PALACE

The basic architectural structures of the park occupy the upper terrace. In its eastern part stands the central edifice, the so-called Cottage Palace put up in 1826–29 by Adam Menelaws. The English name of the palace unusual for the Russia ear, its location in a remote corner of the park, its small dimensions as well as the features of its architectural design and inner decor testify to the new function of the building – this is a place of private habitation rather than a formal state residence. After the construction had been completed, Nicholas I presented the Cottage to Alexandra Fiodorovna and therefore the estate received the name of "Her Majesty's Own Dacha Alexandria".

The architectural and decorative design of the Cottage Palace was carried out in the English Gothic manner imitating the medieval European traditions and known as the Neo- or Pseudo-Gothic style.

The Cottage is a compact, clearly designed two-storey building with a mezzanine. All its fronts have a three-partite articulation. There are elements protruding from the walls – the semi-circle granite porch, covered balconies, terraces and bay windows. The palace is surrounded on all sides with openwork cast-iron arcades – Adam Menelaws was the first to use cast iron as a structural and decorative material in the design of the façades on such a large scale.

The decoration of the interiors of the Cottage was entrusted to the best Russian and Western European masters. Sketches of the famous decorator Giovanni Scotti were used in 1828 to embellish the State Staircase, the ceiling of the Large Study, the Maritime Study and the walls of the Vestibule. The artist Vasily Dodonov adorned the ceiling borders on the first floor and the mezzanine

◀ *I. Vitali. Statue: The Virgin and Child. 1844*

rooms "in the Gothic taste". Adam Menelaws created ornamental compositions of the ceilings reproducing the rose window patterns of Gothic cathedrals and the motifs of richly developed Gothic rose and grilles. The stucco work of the friezes and cornices in the form of vines, oak twigs and arcature fillets, the coat of arms of Alexandria and wrought-iron elements on the façades and in the interiors were executed from models by Mikhail Sokolov. The window and door surrounds in oak and ash carved with alternating garlands of flowers, fruit and leaves were produced by the artist V. Zakharov in 1828–29. The seven fireplaces of white Carrara, yellow Sienese and green Genoese marble as well as the marble floors of the Vestibule and State Staircase were made by the Italian sculptors of the Triscorni family in their St Petersburg workshop. The parquet floors with a simple yet elegant geometric patterns were produced by the well-known master craftsmen A. Tarasov and M. Znamensky.

On the wall of the Vestibule painted in imitation of marble is the shell of a giant tortoise bearing the arms of Alexandria – a sword within a wreath of roses on a blue shield and the motto: "For the faith, the Tsar and the Fatherland". Once the shield was put at the entrance to the park as a sign that the Imperial family was staying in the palace. The motif of White Rose incorporated into the coat

The Small Study. W. Hau.
Portrait of Empress
Alexandra Fiodorovna. 1834

The Vestibule. Tortoise-shell board
with the coat of arms of Alexandria

of arms is recurrent in the decor of the Cottage Palace and its items of decorative and applied art. The poetic name "White Rose" had been given to Princess Charlotte in her childhood (that was the heroine's name in the romance *Der Zauberring* by the German writer Friedrich Heinrich Karl Fouqué de La Motte).

The centerpiece in the layout of the palace and the vertical axis of the building around which are symmetrically grouped the rooms on all the storeys is the Main Staircase.

The Main Staircase and its decor were manufactured of cast-iron at the Alexandrovsky Cast-Iron Works in St Petersburg. The walls of the staircase were painted in grisaille (a kind of painting imitating three-dimensional sculptural or architectural forms in shades of one colour) after sketches by Giovanni Scotti in warm light brown tones against a blue background. The perspective painted decoration creates an amazing illusionary effect seemingly moving the walls of the narrow staircase flight apart and arising a sense of spatial depth and upward thrust which were typical of Gothic architecture.

271

The infatuation with Gothic is also reflected in the subject matter of pictures which are hung in the Small Study: for example, Franz Krüger's watercolour of 1829 shows the Prussian Prince William, brother of Empress Alexandra Fiodorovna, as a knight bound in armour, and a portrait executed by the court painter Timofei Neff in the late 1830s features Olga Nikolayevna, Nicholas I's daughter, the future Queen of Württemberg, in a medieval costume against a lancet window.

On the writing desk stands a portrait of Alexandra Fiodorovna depicted in the Study by Woldemar Hau in 1834. The room contains many personal belongings of Alexandra Fiodorovna, presents, souvenirs and family relics. The Prussian court jeweller Johann

◄ *A. Briullov. Portrait of Alexandra Fiodorovna in the Drawing-Room of the Cottage Palace. 1830*

Rose bush in a pot. Berlin, Germany. By J. G. Hossauer. 1852

Georg Hossauer in 1852 made for Alexandra Fiodorovna in 1830 the so-called "Potsdam Goblet", a silver vessel bearing enamel representations of the arms of participants in the "Magic of the White Rose" tournament held at Potsdam in her honour in 1829. On the table is an exquisite mother-of-pearl clock in the form of rose. A twig of silver roses, also a work by Hossauer (1829), can be seen on a shelf. In 1852 Hossauer created for Alexandra Fiodorovna a rose bush of silver and ormolu.

The Potsdam Goblet. Berlin, Germany. By J. G. Hossauer. 1830

273

The Drawing-Room is the central room of the ground floor. Its huge bay windows and paned balcony doors link the interior of the "rural house" with the surrounding natural environment. The jardinières woven with greenery, the garlands of creepers, flowers on the windows, vases with bouquets of garden and wild flowers create an illusion of a country life.

Objects of decorative and applied art play a great role in the image of the Drawing-Room. A real masterpiece is a set of candelabra and clock in the form of the façade of Rouen Cathedral made by the Russian master craftsmen at the Imperial Porcelain Factory in the 1830s. Set on the mantelpiece are a pair of vases produced at the Sèvres Porcelain Factory in the 1800s. The vases are decorated with painted designs on subjects borrowed from Virgil's poem *Georgica*. Presented to Alexander I by Napoleon in 1807, during the signing of the Treaty of Tilsit, they were preserved in the Cottage Palace as a memory of Nicholas I's elder brother. On the walls of the Drawing-Room are canvases by French landscape painters of the Romantic trend – Théodore Gudin and Philippe Tanneur – as well as a number of early works by Ivan Aivazovsky: *Venice* (1842), a pair of genre Oriental Scenes (1846) and *A View of the Stock Exchange in St Petersburg* (1847).

The decor and the furnishings of the Library are distinguished by a rare unity of style. Everything here is sustained in the Gothic taste: the huge bookcase covering the whole wall and reminiscent of the choirs of a medieval cathedral, a screen made in Germany in the nineteenth century and featuring ladies and cavaliers in medieval garments. The paintings show interiors of medieval monasteries and scenes of medieval life. The book collection of the Cottage Palace amounted to some 1000 volumes by all famous writers of the Romantic trend in English, French, German and Italian. A place of honour was given in the Library to the volumes of poetry by Vasily Zhukovsky who introduced Alexandra Fiodorovna to the Russian language, literature and history and who later became the main tutor of the heir, the future Tsar-Liberator Alexander II. It was Zhukovsky who designed the coat of arms of the Alexandria.

An interesting feature of the Library is the 1846 painting by Fiodor Moller which is based on the subject of Alexander Pushkin's *Eugene Onegin*. It features Tatyana writing her letter to Onegin.

The Drawing-Room

275

The book collection of the Cottage Palace also included popular editions for family reading – keepsakes or de luxe editions richly illustrated with engravings, books on history, geography, religion, genealogy, army and naval regulations, and *The Complete Collection of Laws of the Russian Empire* compiled and systematized on the orders of Nicholas I in 1833.

The Large Reception Room fnctioned as one more drawing-room or was used for a family repose. A notable feature of this interior is the stove embellished by Giovanni Scotti with painted architectural elements: the tracery of a Gothic window and a pattern of the cast-iron arcades skirting the building.

One of the most valuable works of decorative art represented in the Cottage Palace is the silver chandelier shaped as an openwork basket for flowers entwined with twigs bearing twenty-five roses. The chandelier made by Johann Georg Hossauer from a drawing by the Empress's brother, Frederick William IV, the King of Prussia, was presented to Alexandra Fiodorovna and Nicholas I on the occasion of their silver marriage by their German relatives in 1842. The Large Reception Room is adorned with landscapes by the best Russian painters of the Romantic trend. Over the doors are two *Views of Odessa* (1929) by Maxim Vorobyev and a unique

The Library. F. Moller.
Tatyana Writing a Letter to Onegin. 1846

landscape by Orest Kiprensky, *A View of Mt Vesuvius* (1831), permeated with an anxious, sombre mood. On the walls are the seascape *A View of Amalfi Bay* by Sylvester Shchedrin (1826) and two marinas by Ivan Aivazovsky – *A View of the Crimea* (1852) and *A View of Oreanda in the Crimea* (1858).

In 1842 a special "dining room" and an open marble terrace were annexed to the east front of the palace. The annex was connected with the earlier part of the building by an impressive lancet arch. Nearby, in a recess of the wall, the statue *The Madonna and Child* (1844) by Ivan Vitali can be seen.

The Dining-Room was usually used for private meals in a narrow circle; not frequently persons from the Imperial family's closest entourage were invited.

In the centre of the Dining-Room stands Her Majesty's Own Service for twenty-four diners produced in the late 1820s – early 1830s at the Imperial Porcelain Factory and the Imperial Glass

The Drawing-Room. The Rouen Cathedral
clock and candelabra. The Imperial
Porcelain Factory, St Petersburg. 1830

The Library ▶

◀ The Dining-Room

The Large Reception Room.
S. Shchedrin. View
of the Amalfi Bay. 1826

The Large Reception Room.
I. Aivazovsky. View of the Crimea. 1852

Works specially for the Cottage Palace. The service includes snow-white porcelain articles of simple and austere forms, crystal glass vessels with diamond-faceted decoration and glassware of ruby, cobalt, opal and emerald colours.

The walls of the room are embellished with paintings by Ivan Aivazovsky. Noteworthy among them is the large-scale painting *View of Constantinople at Sunset* (1846). Also displayed in the room are pictures by masters of the "Italian genre" – Pimen Orlov, Timofei Neff and Sokrat Vorobyev. Of special historical interest are three panoramic views by Théodore Gudin featuring the Alexandria Park at different times of day. They were commissioned from the artist by Nicholas I in 1841.

Usually the Small Reception Room functioned as the place where courtiers and maids of honour were waiting for the Empress's orders.

The room was decorated in the middle of the nineteenth century in the Neo-Rococo style, which revived the mid-eighteenth century Rococo shapes a century later. The corbels are used as supports for a small but valuable collection of porcelain statuettes created in the nineteenth century after models by the famous eighteenth-century masters Johann Kändler and Michel Victor Acier at the Meissen Porcelain Factory.

On the pedestal stands a bronze bust of Alexandra Fiodorovna cast in 1841 by Peter Klodt from Christian Rauch's model of 1826.

The rooms of the children and of Nicholas I were on the first floor. On the walls of the Heir's Training Room are engraved portraits of members of the Imperial family.

Worthy of attention among objects of daily use is a gilt bronze casket inlaid with malachite, lapis lazuli, agate, semiprecious stones and strasses. The casket was used to keep the baptismal accessories of the heir – his shirt, cap, etc.

In the Large Study Nicholas I used to receive reports of ministers and generals and the commandant of Peterhof. On the writing tables are ink sets, stamps of rock crystal and topaz bearing the coat of arms of Alexandria, a small state stamp, a paper weight, bells and other objects related to the Emperor's activities. A tribute to the memory of Peter the Great was the decoration of the walls with paintings

The Dining-Room. I. Aivazovsky.
View of the Neapolitan Bay. 1841

The Large Study

by the Small Dutch Masters of the seventeenth and eighteenth centuries which Nicholas I himself chose from the collection of the Imperial Hermitage. These are works by Adam Silo, the marine painters Jan van Goyen, Julius Porcellis, Arent Arentsz, Simon de Vlieger, Ludolf Backhuysen and others.

Next to the Study are rooms of the Emperor's daughters. In the room of Maria Nikolayevna, the Emperor's eldest daughter, has retained its original decoration, which is simple and unpretentious like in all the rooms of the first floor. There are several portraits of Nicholas I on display here. The large painting by Yegor Botman (1849) features the Emperor with his favourite dog Hussar against the background of the Cottage Palace. A highlight of the interior and of the palace as a whole is a unique clock showing the time in sixty-six towns of Russia including that in Mos-

cow, St Petersburg and New Archangel at Alaska. It was made by the clock-maker Ivan Yurin in 1861.

Under the roof of the palace is the second storey with the Maritime Study of Nicholas I with the adjacent balcony affording a fine view of the expanses of the Gulf of Finland. The decor of the Maritime Study resembles a military tent – its walls and ceiling seem to be covered with fabric arranged in folds and rich draperies executed in silvery, grey, blue and ochreous tones and embellished with small flowers and the arms of Alexandria.

The walls of the Maritime Study are hung with engraved and painted seascapes including *A Seaside View* (1849) by Ivan Aivazovsky. On the desk are placed maritime instruments – telescopes, a compass, a sundial, a geodesic device and a silver megaphone of Nicholas I.

◀ *The Room of Maria Nikolayevna. Ye. Botman.*
Portrait of Emperor Nicholas I. 1849

Strelna

Strelna is situated on the south shore of the Gulf of Finland, 22.5 kilometres from St Petersburg. Strelna is remarkable not only for its location and beautiful landscapes, but also for its majestic palace and park complex of the eighteenth and nineteenth centuries which has an original layout, unusual appearance and a long history. It consists of two complexes: the formal one, with the stone Konstantin Palace and a regular park as its landmarks and an earlier one, notable for the wooden Palace of Peter the Great. The layout of the Strelna gardens and parks is oriented towards the Gulf of Finland. Strelna, like Peterhof, is a seaside residence. In the eighteenth century it belonged the royal family and in the nineteenth, to the grand dukes, Konstantin's sons.

Strelna is one of the most ancient settlements on the south bank of the Gulf of Finland. In the eighth and ninth centuries these lands were inhabited by the Russians. Later the settlements of the peoples of the Finno-Ugric group appeared, who, like the Russian inhabitants, were subjects of the Novgorod Republic. In 1624 Strelna became the property of Johan Skytte, a well-known Swedish enlightener and statesman.

The Study. Unknown painter of the early 18th century.
Portrait of Peter the Great

Soon after the victorious Battle of Poltava of 1709 Peter the Great decided to start an improvement of the areas around the future capital of the Empire. The Tsar ordered Alexander Menshikov, his closest associate, to build a couple of huts, a cattle-yard, an aviary and a small fish pond at Strelna. The designer of the initial project of the Palace of Peter the Great is unknown. Its construction had been finished by 1716, and in 1719–20 it was rebuilt on the order of the Tsar.

Peter's ensemble includes: the Palace of Peter the Great, the green garden with two fountains and the Fruit Garden.

The Palace of Peter the Great has a three-partite design: to the central two-storey volume completed by the triangular pediment are attached two wings. The palace is adorned by a six-column portico supporting a balcony and lending the building an imposing view. The architects who created the palace skillfully blended it with the environment. The main façade of the palace overlooks the sea. It produces a monumental impression on the north side – its height is largely enhanced by the natural slope of the hill. The architectural solution of the south façade, extended along the hill in a line, is marked by a more modest decor.

Vegetables and fruits from the Strelna kitchen-garden

The Dining-Room

Its horizontal extension is emphasized by the clear-cut rhythm of the windows with small panes; the central part of the building is singled out by an attic storey and a porch with four steps.

On the north side of the Palace of Peter the Great is a garden with two fountains laid out on the green slope of a hill. The Fruit Garden was also called the Upper or Berry Garden. It is known that during the age of Peter the Great a number of greenhouses were built on the estate in which fig-, peach- and apricot-trees, wild oranges, laurels, various kinds of flowers and herbs were grown.

Throughout the eighteenth century the Palace of Peter the Great was used as a stopping place for temporary accommodation – it served for brief stays and repose of the Russian monarchs on their way from St Petersburg to Kronstadt, Peterhof or Oranienbaum. On stopping at the Palace of Peter the Great near the Peterhof road, the Russian Emperors and Empresses left their chests, caskets and others things in the Travel Room. Displayed in the centre of this room is Emperor Alexander III's travelling chest, a characteristic item of palatial everyday life in the eighteenth and nineteenth centuries. Such chests were usually taken for travelling tours or military campaigns, for troop exercises or reviews which would last longer than a single day.

Leaving the city for a travelling tour or campaign, for a military reviewing or training, which would last more than a single day, members of the royal family used to take with them travelling chests in which they could keep all the necessities.

When folded, the Emperor's chest has a rectangular shape with a convex cover; it is provided with metal handles and buckles for securing belts. Its wooden body is lined with dense crude cloth inside and bound with iron sheets and metal strips outside. The chest has four compartments: one below, two in the middle and one at the top.

The top compartment has several sections used to keep personal hygienic belongings, the same compartment includes sections for keeping headgear, epaulettes, shoulder-belts, tobacco and cigarettes. There are also accessories for stretching gloves, a candle lamp and a homeopathic pharmacy. The middle compartment of the chest contains a bedstead frame in the shape of folding wooden rails with two

*The Travel Room. A set of of writing
instruments of Emperor Alexander III*

feet. The lower compartment of the chest has three drawers: one is intended for linen and two for vessels.

The corner room known as the "Fortune Parlour", was intended for pastimes. The Russian Emperors and Empresses used to spend time in the company of their closest associates and guests there.

On display in the Fortune Parlour are a carved wooden set of chess, draughts, ivory "spills" for playing spillikins, dominoes, Roulette (called then *fortunka* in Russia), cards and various accessories for playing cards. On the south wall of the Fortune Parlour is a *Portrait of the Jester Balakirev* by an anonymous eighteenth-century painter.

The Dining-Room is the largest interior on the ground floor of the palace. Displayed on the large table in the Dining-Room is a porcelain tea service for six diners executed in the 1750s at the Meissen Royal Factory. It includes a set of cups and saucers, a teapot, a sugar-bowl and other items with an overglaze painted decoration featuring ladies and gentlemen in a landscape setting. The representations are placed in reserves encircled with golden frames.

Represented in the Dining-Room is a unique brass samovar with a silver coating produced in the second half of the eighteenth century by Russian master craftsmen. It has an ornate band of pierced representations of playing cards and is provided with two taps, over which an engraved monogram of Catherine the Great in an oval medallion can be seen. Tradition has it that this samovar was served to Catherine the Great when she was engaged in card playing.

The Passage Room. J. C. Seekatz. Boy with a Brazier. ▶
Germany. Mid-18th century

The Fortune Parlour. Unknown artist of the 18th century.
Portrait of the Jester Balakirev

Seekatz. The Drawing-Room is remarkable for the clock, with its movement, weights and pendulum in a wooden case, made by the eminent Amsterdam master Willem Coster in the 1730s. The clock marks, in addition to hours and minutes, dates, months, week-days and moon phases. On the walls are *The Holy Family on the Way to Egypt*, a signed work by the Flemish painter Pieter van Bloemen, *Landscape with a Herd*, a painting by the Dutch artist Pieter Symonsz Potter, and a canvas by an unknown seventeenth-century Flemish painter, *The Antique Room*.

The Study is the last room of the ground floor. The pattern of alternating white and yellow strips characteristic of the Study's wallpaper serves as a beautiful background for

The Bedroom. Costume of Peter the Great. 1710s–1720s

The decor of the bedroom has a memorial character. The large canopied bed, upholstered and draped with dark green woollen fabric called *flachtuch*, is covered with a patchwork quilt which was sewn for the Tsar, as legend has it, by his wife Catherine I. The glazed showcase displays an everyday costume of Peter the Great cut according to the European fashion of the 1710s and 1720s: it consists of a juste-au-corps and culottes sewn of a brown cloth and embroidered in light brown silk, with buttons braided with the same silk thread.

The historically unique objects of the palace include Peter's screen which separated the bed from the rest of the room. Datable to the first quarter of the eighteenth century, it is bound with stamped leather and decorated with polychrome painting in the chinoiserie style testifying to European artists' interest in Chinese art. Earlier this screen was at the Peterhof palace of Monplaisir. Such screens were usually used as a protection against draughts.

In the Passage Room is one of the best paintings of Peter the Great's collection – *Boy with a Brazier* by the German painter Johann Conrad

The Bedroom ▶

292

engravings representing the European monarchs, predecessors and contemporaries of Peter the Great. On the north wall is the formal portrait of Peter the Great. This is a rare likeness of the young Tsar painted from life by an unknown artist of the late seventeenth century. The west wall of the Study is adorned with a bronze bas-relief bearing a portrait of Peter the Great by Bartolomeo Carlo Rastrelli. Under the bas-relief is a bronze copy from a cast of Peter the Great's hand made at the Milovanov Brothers Factory. The formal character of the interior is emphasized by its furniture: Dutch carved chairs, an elegant oak armchair decorated with carving, network ornament and an inlay of walnut and mahogany, as well as two cabinets. The trimming of one cabinet veneered with ebony and inlaid with ivory and tortoise-shell is especially exquisite. Such cabinets began to be delivered to Russia from Europe in the late seventeenth century.

The Upper Hall is the biggest room in the palace: it occupies an area of 85 square metres. The Upper Hall was intended for formal receptions, dinners, balls and other ceremonial occasions. The walls of the Hall are decorated with paintings by Western European masters of various schools and genres.

The Upper Hall houses an interesting collection of Chinese and Japanese vases of the eighteenth and nineteenth centuries. The card tables placed near the walls are used to display various porcelain pieces manufactured at the Meissen Factory. Shown here are allegories of the parts of the world, figures of ladies and gentlemen, pastoral scenes and mythological creatures. The groups *Bacchus and Venus*, *Europa* and *Shepherdess and Her Cavalier* executed in the 1740s after models by Johann Joachim Kändler are decorated with bright painting of contrasting tones. The group *Asia and Africa* in the form of two embracing children was produced in 1755 after a model by Friedrich Elias Meyer. The festive character of the interior is emphasized by two bronze sculptural groups devoted to mythological subjects, *Apollo and Daphne* by the Italian sculptor Giovanni Foggini, cast in the 1720s, and *Vertumnus and Pomona* by the French sculptor Robert Le Lorrain, dated 1704.

The Upper Hall

J. J. Meyer 1811

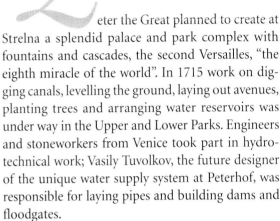

Peter the Great planned to create at Strelna a splendid palace and park complex with fountains and cascades, the second Versailles, "the eighth miracle of the world". In 1715 work on digging canals, levelling the ground, laying out avenues, planting trees and arranging water reservoirs was under way in the Upper and Lower Parks. Engineers and stoneworkers from Venice took part in hydrotechnical work; Vasily Tuvolkov, the future designer of the unique water supply system at Peterhof, was responsible for laying pipes and building dams and floodgates.

Peter the Great commissioned designs of the palace and park ensemble from the best architects of the period – Bartolomeo Carlo Rastrelli, Jean-Baptiste Le Blond, Sebastiano Cipriani, Niccolo Michetti – and approved only the latter's project.

In 1719 work on parterres, a cross canal and diagonal prospects began in the Lower Park. On 22 June 1720 a stone palace with triple arched span in the central part of the building and with a grotto was founded. The work on the Strelna complex, however, was suspended as it was impossible to create highspurting fountains.

The construction started at Strelna by Peter the Great was continued during the reign of his daughter, Elizabeth Petrovna. In the middle of the eighteenth century the architect Francesco Bartolomeo Rastrelli completed the façades of the stone palace.

In 1797 Paul I presented the farmstead Strelna with 149 serfs and all the villages assigned to it to his second son, Grand Duke Konstantin (1779–1831).

*J. Meyer. View of the Great Palace
at Strelna. 1811*

Ivanov from the watercolour by V. Sadovnikov.
View of the Great Palace at Strelna.1833

The architect Andrei Voronikhin reconstructed the stone palace in 1802–03 and Luigi Rusca restored it in 1804, after a fire. The grand duke used the restored palace to accommodate the headquarters, arsenal, hospital, guardhouse and stables of the Uhlan regiment.

After his death the Strelna estate was in the possession of Grand Duke Konstatin Nikolayevich (1827–1892), Nicholas I's second son. Before he attained majority, Strelna had been under the jurisdiction of the Department of Crown Domains, and in summertime various regiments quartered there, including the Mounted Regiment of Life-Guards.

In 1848 the grand duke obtained possession of all rights for Strelna. He received the estate as a present for his marriage to Grand Duchess Alexandra Iosifovna, née Princess of Saxe-Altenburg. By the arrival of the young couple a restoration and redesigning of the grottoes in the Lower Park, the building of the Stable and a reconstruction of the stone palace, which became known as the "Konstantin Palace" had been completed according to designs by Christoph Philip Meyer and Andrei Stackenschneider.

In 1853 the grand duke was put at the head of the Naval Ministry where he made a series of positive changes and reforms.

A. Orlowski. Portrait of Grand Duke ▶
Konstantin Pavlovich. 1802
The State Russian Museum, St Petersburg

Unknown artist. His Imperial Highness
Grand Duke Konstantin Nikolayevich
as the Most August Colonel-in-Chief
of the Life-Guards Finland Regiment. 1880s

P. Cherkasov. The Great
Palace at Strelna. 1855

The Konstantin Palace – The Palace of Congresses

He took an active part in the preparation of the reform on the abolition of serfdom and in 1865 became the Chairman of the State Council. In 1881, after the assassination of Emperor Alexander II, Konstantin Nikolayevich resigned from all the posts retaining only the honourary title of General-Admiral. He died in 1892, in Pavlovsk.

The Konstantin Palace served as the dwelling place of Grand Duke Konstantin Nikolayevich for 43 years. The most august owner left to his descendants a well-equipped estate meeting the up-to-date demands of comfort: the palace with imposing state rooms and halls encircled by gardens with picturesque ponds and cool tufa grottoes, terraces adorned with flowerbeds as well as marble and bronze statuary. Thanks to the grand duke the former farmstead Strelna turned into a fashionable place of summer rest.

After the death of Konstantin Nikolayevich, from 1892 to 1911, the estate was owned by Grand Duchess Alexandra Iosifovna.

The last owner of Strelna was Grand Duke Dmitry Konstantinovich (1860–1919), the junior son of Grand Duke Konstantin Nikolayevich. He was born in 1860 in the Konstantin Palace. He was appointed the commander of a regiment of mounted grenadiers and remained on this post until 1917 rising to the rank of colonel. Dmitry Konstantinovich is also known for his charity activities. Under his august patronage were the society Brotherhood for One's Neighbour, a surgery, a hospital and a fire brigade founded at Strelna. After the revolution of 1917 the grand duke was arrested and shot in the Peter and Paul Fortress in 1919.

The life and creative work of Grand Duke Konstantin Konstantinovich (1858–1915), the second son of Konstantin Nikolayevich, eminent poet (he signed his works by the initials, *K. R.*, standing for "Konstantin Romanov") was closely linked with Strelna where he was born and spent his childhood and youth. Wherever his destiny brought him, he always remembered his native land and carried with himself a metal box with the earth taken at Strelna.

CONCLUSION

Peterhof is a gem of Russia, a vivid symbol of the blend of European and Russian culture. Millions of guests visit this world-famous museum-preserve enjoying the magnificent decor of the palaces and the refined beauty of the parks stretching on the sea-shore. Every spring a brilliant festival devoted to the opening of the Peterhof fountains is held and in late autumn, when twilight falls on the splendid royal residence, the sky is illuminated by picturesque fireworks. At Peterhof, which will celebrate its centenary in 2005, the most interesting pages in Russian history seem to come to life.

P E T E R H O F

Authors N. Vernova and V. Znamenov

General manager of the project L. Pantina

Designed by A. Pompeev

Edited by A. Barkhatova

Translated from the Russian by V. Fateyev

Photographs by L. Bogdanov, V. Dorokhov, A. Ivanov, L. Kheifets,
B. Manushin, V. Melnikov, Yu. Molodkovets, Ye. Pantin, A. Pompeev,
G. Shablovsky, V. Vereshchagin, V. Vorontsov, V. Yegorovsky

Computer preparation of the material by
A. Pompeev and A. Yarilov

Abris Publishers thank the researchers
of the Peterhof State Museum-Reserve
N. Fediushina, O. Kislitsina, T. Nosovich,
M. Obaturova, M. Platonova, G. Schultz, V. Tenikhina,
M. Trubanovskaya and V. Yumangulov
for participating in the preparation of this book

Almanac "Treasures of Russia"
Issue 56

№ П 2462 от 30.04.97 в СЗРУ Госкомпечати РФ

Тираж 2500. Цена договорная

ISBN 5-88810-064-1

Printed in Libris OY, Finland,
www.libris.fi

Abris Art Publishers – tel. (812) 934-74-95, 951-35-50,
E-mail: pompeev@mail.convey.ru

DEDICATED
TO THE 300TH ANNIVERSARY
OF ST PETERSBURG

1705 to 2005